Sarum Chronicle ISSUE THREE

Contents

Sarum Chronicle is published on behalf of its editorial team by Hobnob Press, P O Box 1838, East Knoyle, Salisbury SP3 6FA, to whom all orders, correspondence and contributions for future issues should be addressed. Potential contributors are invited to apply for a style sheet.

Front cover illustration: The statue of Henry Fawcett in Salisbury market place. See p 3. (photograph by Joe Newman)

Introduction

This is the third issue of *Sarum Chronicle,* by now well established in the Salisbury area as a worthy successor to the *Hatcher Review.* Again the contents reflect varied research interests over a wide spectrum of history.

Dr Carrie Smith has produced an authoritative and surprising account of justice in late medieval Salisbury, where the law was manipulated to achieve what was considered an equitable result. Don Cross, a local expert on industrial archaeology and tourism, has traced the history of the ill-fated Avon Navigation from Salisbury to Christchurch. Peter Fawcett has added a personal touch with his article on his great-great uncle, Henry Fawcett, potentially one of the leading statesmen of the 19th century, but remembered in Salisbury today primarily for his statue in the Market Square. Dr John Elliott was a contributor to *Sarum Chronicle 2*. His new paper on fallen women in Salisbury not only reflects contemporary Victorian and later attitudes, but provides information on a neglected area of Salisbury local history. Peter Barrie's contribution on the building of a new parish church to serve the rapidly growing late-Victorian suburb of St Mark's, is also a little known story. How different St Mark's would have looked with a tower, as its architect, J Arthur Reeve, envisaged! There are also briefer contributions on the history of Salisbury's fine amateur drama group, Studio Theatre; on the naming of roads on Bishopdown; and on a newly discovered Salisbury working-class memoir.

Contributions to future issues of *Sarum Chronicle* are always appreciated – articles, short notes and comments, book reviews. Suggestions would be welcome for establishing a series on local archive material, perhaps a letter, cartoon, diary entry, photograph, playbill which relates to the history of Salisbury or a neighbouring village. Brief guidelines are available for those wishing to write articles and may be obtained from one of the editorial team or via Hobnob Press.

The editorial team of John Chandler, Jane Howells, Sue Johnson, Ruth Newman and Margaret Smith has welcomed a new member, John Elliott, an authority on Victorian art and architecture and a contributor to our current issue. With this additional help, and in order to increase further the circulation of *Sarum Chronicle* to ensure its continued success, we are planning to establish a subscription list (with the option of payment by standing order or invoice). Membership of the list will guarantee your copy of each newly published issue at the special discounted price for subscribers. Please indicate your interest by completing the enclosed form and return it promptly to Hobnob Press.

Henry Fawcett, 1833 – 1884

Peter Fawcett

Nearly 150 years ago on a glorious Autumn day, 18 September 1858, a group of men – a shooting party – was walking along the top of Harnham Hill. The view from the hill then must have been even more spectacular than it is today. Harnham was still a tiny village on the bank of the Avon, and beyond the river the open meadows stretched back to our magnificent cathedral. The men paused to take in the scene and then proceeded on their way in search of game. Among them were two well-known members of the local community: William Fawcett, past mayor of Salisbury and a leading light in the local Liberal party, and his son, Henry.

As they were crossing a field a partridge was put to flight, William Fawcett raised his shotgun and fired, failing to notice his son standing ahead of him and slightly to his right. A number of stray pellets hit the younger man. Most bounced harmlessly off his chest but two smashed through his spectacles to blind him instantly. He was 25 years old.

If Henry Fawcett is remembered at all it is for being the blind Postmaster General. His statue stands in Salisbury's market square, tall and green in the dappled sunlight; its sightless eyes watch the generations come and go – a reminder of a man who is almost forgotten. Yet there is no doubt that he was potentially one of the great statesmen of the nineteenth century and probably one of the first true Social Democrats. And it is entirely appropriate that his likeness graces the centre of our city, for this is where Henry Fawcett MP was born on the 26 August 1833 – in an Elizabethan room above his father's shop overlooking the market place.

William, Henry's father, was originally a Westmorland man but had spent three fruitless years trying to survive in London before arriving in Salisbury during 1815. He worked for Mr Pinkney who ran a draper's shop; William took over the business upon his employer's retirement and prospered. In 1824 he married Mary Cooper, the daughter of a local solicitor who also acted as agent for the local Liberal party, and they had four children, three boys and a girl. In 1832, the year before Henry's birth, William had been elected Mayor of Salisbury.

The family had a house in the city centre until 1841, when the Earl of Radnor offered them the lease of the Home Farm at Longford. Shortly after this, eight-year-old Henry was enrolled as a boarder at Mr Sopp's school in Alderbury, where he studied for six years. Then he became the first pupil at Mr Edmonson's Queenwood College (previously called Harmony Hall) where he developed his talents for mathematics and public speaking. Eighteen months later he moved to King's College School in London. His father, although prosperous, was not a rich man and was concerned how best to further Henry's education upon leaving King's College. William consulted his close friend the Dean of Salisbury who judged the 19 year old's impressive mathematical achievements worthy of a place at Cambridge.

Henry's own excellent education did not blind him to the realities of those less fortunate. During his holidays from school he had formed close friendships with many of the workers on the Longford Estate. Countryside children from poor families were lucky to be taught anything – working the land to survive was their priority. Henry was coming to believe strongly that the best way to help them lay in education – education for all – irrespective of religious beliefs, gender or social standing. Education helps people to help themselves: a simple principle which would profoundly influence his political philosophies and thinking in later life.

Cambridge in those days was a hotbed of political radicalism and debate. Henry went to Peterhouse and his early time there seems to have been filled with great happiness and intense learning. Being gregarious he made friends easily, and he participated in sports although never with any great success. A close follower of John Stuart Mill, the eminent political economist, Henry soon established himself as one of the leading speakers of the Debating Club, known as the 'Union'. His second year saw him in Trinity Hall as a pensioner, which relieved his parents of some of the financial strain. In 1856 he tried for the 'Senior Wranglership' but failed. However, later the same year he was elected to a fellowship of his college, gaining honour and a further £250 per annum. Henry knew he must be responsible for his own income once his studies ended, so, while still at Cambridge, he entered Lincoln's Inn to study for the bar.

Unfortunately this coincided with deteriorating eyesight (which seems ironic considering the affliction to befall him shortly). He consulted a number of specialists and the consensus was that he must stop reading for at least a year. Taking this advice to heart he returned home to his family in Longford. He and his sister Maria had always been devoted to each other and she spent many hours reading aloud and taking dictation of the numerous letters that he wrote to friends. To one he wrote:

> I regard you with such true affection that I have long wished to impart my mind on many subjects. You know somewhat of my character; you shall now hear my views as to my future. I started life as a boy with the ambition some day to enter the House of Commons. Every effort, every endeavour, which I have ever put

forth has had this object in view. I have continually tried, and shall, I trust, still try not only honourably to gratify my desire, but also to fit myself for such an important trust. I feel that I ought to make any sacrifice, to endure any amount of labour, to obtain this position, because every day I become more deeply impressed with the powerful conviction that this is the position in which I could be of the greatest use to my fellow men, and that I could in the House of Commons exert an influence in removing the social evils of our country, and especially the paramount one – the mental degradation of millions.

Shortly after this letter was written he went shooting with his father and tragedy struck.

The words Henry spoke immediately after the accident were said to be 'This will make no difference'. What is confirmed is that on his return to Longford his first words were, 'Read the newspaper to me, Maria'. There was great despair in the Fawcett household. William, Henry's father, was inconsolable with guilt and Henry's mother locked herself away. It was left to Maria, Henry's sister, to hold the family together during those terrible weeks after the shooting. Through it all Henry never once complained although, as he lay in bed, his private feelings of despair can only be imagined: an unsuccessful eye operation only confirmed that his life would be spent in darkness. He received many letters of condolence, most of which made him feel even more depressed until one arrived from his Cambridge friend and mentor Professor Hopkins. Wasting no words on sympathy he urged Henry to make use of his academic and intellectual gifts by returning to Cambridge. This letter more than anything else seems to have lifted his spirit and determined him to pursue his life's ambition despite his blindness – to be a Member of Parliament.

Very soon he was up and walking, often accompanied by Maria or one of his brothers. His sister numbered all his clothes and he was able to select his own wardrobe simply by instructing her which numbers he wanted to wear. And then he was dining out again, going horse riding, and, one of his favourite pastimes, salmon fishing. Life was there to be embraced, accident or no – to the extent of mountain climbing in Wales and even ice-skating regularly on the frozen Cambridgeshire fens and Norfolk Broads.

After being blinded, Henry quit law and returned to Trinity Hall at Cambridge where he grew more politically active. In 1860 he put himself forward as the prospective Liberal candidate for Southwark, following the death of Admiral Sir Charles Napier, the incumbent Tory member. He had to face the selection committee of the local Liberal party, and there met considerable opposition, both on political grounds due to his Radicalism, and for his blindness. Though he put his message across forcefully enough in public and committee meetings he realised that the antagonism was too strong and he retired from the race.

Henry Fawcett with his father

In 1863 he stood again as Liberal candidate, this time for Cambridge, but lost by a mere 81 votes. He also published his *Manual of Political Economy*, which swiftly established itself as the standard reference work for years to come and paved the way to the post of Professor of Political Economy at Cambridge – and another bitter election battle. Not only was his suitability for the role questioned due to his blindness but he was also accused of Radicalism against the established Conservatism of the university. Despite this he was, at 30 years old and against all the odds, elected to the Chair on 28 November that year. His next political foray took place in Brighton and the selection fight was again bruising, but he won despite causing a rift in the local party. This could not save him from losing a by-election but he was confident that these rehearsals would ensure victory in the coming General Election.

Henry's newly found academic authority gave him the platform to speak out on equality for the poor working classes alongside John Stuart Mill, now his friend and an equally outspoken supporter of Lincoln and his Federation in the ongoing American Civil War. Mill had also become closely involved with the infant women's suffrage movement, a cause Henry wholeheartedly endorsed. And it was at a party in Mill's honour, at the Campden Hill home of fellow radical MP Peter Taylor, attended by suffrage supporters – on the very night when the news of Abraham Lincoln's assassination reached London – that Henry met the love of his life. He heard a girlish voice state loudly, 'It would have been better if every crowned head in Europe had been shot, rather than Lincoln'. Struck not only by the voice but by the sentiments expressed he asked his host for an immediate introduction. The speaker's name was Millicent Garrett, she was 18 years old and one of six daughters of Mr Newson Garrett, a wealthy businessman of Aldeburgh, Suffolk.

There are different interpretations about what happened next. One suggestion is that it was Elizabeth, Millicent's elder sister, whom Henry first met through mutual friends. As Elizabeth Garrett Anderson, she would become the country's first ever woman doctor. Another school of thought maintains that Millicent was the introduction to her elder sister. Elizabeth and Henry were of similar age and their friendship quickly ripened. On the 8 May 1865 Elizabeth wrote to her parents stating that Henry had proposed and that she had turned him down saying that her work would make marriage impossible. None the less she may have had a twinge of regret. Her letter continued:

> I have not the least doubt about having been right in decidedly refusing though at the same time I know of few lives I should have liked better than being eyes and hands to a Cambridge Professor and an MP.

Elizabeth's rejection of Henry's proposal must have affected him deeply – but there were compensations. On 12 July 1865 he realised part of his dream and was elected as the Member of Parliament for Brighton. Then just over a year later, in October 1866 he became engaged to Millicent, Elizabeth's young sister. The initial courtship and engagement were not without problems. The Garretts feared Henry's blindness could handicap their young daughter's future happiness, and, unbeknown to Millicent, the family business was going through a difficult financial time, so a hugely expensive society wedding was not an option. Millicent's parents set a year's separation as a prerequisite of family acceptance. Many people wrote in support of the union but it was Henry who wrote the letter that finally swayed the parents in the young couple's favour. Millicent's mother passed the letter to her daughter who treasured it for the rest of her life.

Henry Fawcett and Millicent Garrett were married in Aldeburgh on 23 April 1867. After the ceremony their honeymoon was to be in a rented cottage in Alderbury. At Waterloo Station they met Sir John Lubbock, a friend from Wiltshire also on the platform waiting for the same train. Henry bundled a protesting Sir John unceremoniously into the flower-decked wedding compart-ment with them to talk politics, much to Millicent's amusement.

They both had well developed senses of fun and enjoyed life. As a joke epitaph written while Henry was still very much alive Millicent penned: 'Here lies the man who found every soup delicious and every woman charming' – which says as much about their relationship as it does about the man. There is a rather touching account of Henry's devotion to his wife which is also in his biography. The many journeys between London, Cambridge and Brighton took their toll. To relax they went riding along the South Downs with friends.

One evening Millicent was thrown violently from her horse and knocked unconscious. Henry's inner strength failed him and he wept inconsolably, refusing to believe his friends' reassurances in the certainty she must be dead. He was so completely overcome that he had to give up an election meeting that evening. The next day he apologised for his absence, saying difficulties were overcome through the help of others and because he had, 'a help-mate whose political judgment was much less frequently at fault than his own' – an attitude to his wife and her opinions which illumined his life.

In turn, her relationship with and subsequent marriage to Henry Fawcett helped form Millicent into the formidable political leader of the non-militant movement for women's suffrage and champion of the working classes. She was made a Dame Grand Cross of the Order of the British Empire in 1924. In 1868 they had a daughter, Philippa, who brought great joy into the couple's life. Philippa inherited her father's remarkable talent for mathematics and was the first woman 'Senior Wrangler' at Cambridge, the highest scoring examinee in mathematics of her year. This was a major triumph both for herself and for the cause of women's emacipation.

Henry and his new wife divided their time between modest homes in London and Cambridge and soon became well known for their hospitality. Henry had always been a very sociable man. Throughout their marriage they also made certain they travelled to Salisbury as often as possible to see Henry's parents, first at Longford then in the Cathedral Close.

After his election to Parliament Henry Fawcett's career proceeded apace. He was tireless in the cause of the working man, fought religious interference in university education, vigorously promoted women's suffrage, and was such a friend to the poor and homeless in India that Westminster nicknamed him 'The Member for India'. He believed a country was best run by its people themselves, and on this subject he made his most famous speech in the Commons on 31 July 1873. He spoke for one hour and forty five minutes on the finances of India and the plight of the poor without once being prompted or helped – one of the finest speeches heard in the House of Commons for years. And he championed one particular cause for which the British people can still be grateful. The Government introduced a bill proposing that all common land including some of our great forests should be enclosed and either divided among the local inhabitants on a one-off basis or sold to property developers for maximum return. During one of his many speeches in the Commons on this subject, he is reported to have quoted the following poem:

> The Law locks up the man or woman
> Who steals the goose from off the common
> But lets the greater villain loose
> Who steals the common from the goose.

Henry Fawcett and his supporters fought this Bill using every parliamentary procedure to frustrate the Whips and because of their opposition a select committee was set up of which he was made a member. Eventually the proposal was altered in such a way to ensure that the majority of common land, including the New Forest, was retained for the use of the people. This, of all his victories, was the one of which he felt most proud.

Being a man of strong principles and great independence Henry, on many an occasion, refused to toe the party line when he disagreed with policy, even helping

The wedding of Henry Fawcett and Millicent Garrett, 1867

to bring down Gladstone's government over the Irish problem. However, despite this, he was admired and respected by the members of the House, irrespective of party. There is no doubt that had he not been blind, Henry Fawcett would have filled a senior cabinet post after the clear Liberal success at the General Election of 1880. The talk was of his being either Secretary of State for Colonial Affairs or possibly Chancellor of the Exchequer. But Gladstone was advised that Henry's blindness was considered a security risk: all state papers however sensitive would have to be read out to him. So instead of being invited to form part of the government Henry Fawcett was appointed Post Master General.

Although greatly honoured to be a Privy Councillor this was a disappointment, but in his usual manner he undertook his duties at the Post Office with determination. First, through consultation at all levels with his staff, the 'whole system was waked up, shaken from its lethargy, and flooded with a new interest'. Second he greatly enhanced the opportunities for women employees.

And then he implemented a five point plan: the provision of a parcel post, introduction of money postal orders, a small-savings bank, a life insurance scheme, and reduced cost telegrams. In addition Fawcett was keen that a new invention called the telephone should be made as widely available as possible.

Henry Fawcett was still dividing his life between his academic position in Cambridge and the public duties of his constituency – but now there was the added stress of heading a huge national institution. In November 1882, after a particularly busy time, he fell ill, was diagnosed with both diphtheria and typhoid and until the end of December his life was in grave danger. During this time, it seems that nearly the whole country was willing him to survive. The Queen telegraphed frequently, sometimes twice a day and, according to reports, Henry Fawcett's illness was the major topic of conversation in the clubs and taverns throughout the Kingdom. By mid-January 1883 he was pronounced out of danger and during February spent a few days of convalescence at his parents house in the Close.

Typically he then launched himself back into intense hard work. In the summer of 1884 commitments prevented the Fawcetts from taking a holiday. On 13 October, Henry made a speech at Hackney and then returned to Cambridge for further lecturing. On 30 October he went to London for parliamentary business and was back in Cambridge again on 2 November, comparing his cold with that of a dinner guest. The following morning he was dangerously ill. Dr Garrett Anderson and a colleague were hastily summoned from London and immediately diagnosed pneumonia. During the afternoon of Thursday 6 November the doctors stepped out of the bedroom to confer. Henry, alone with his wife and daughter complained of feeling cold and said 'The best thing to warm my hands with would be my fur gloves. They are in the pocket of my coat in the dressing room' – his last words. He was 51 years old.

Henry Fawcett's work at the Post Office has been widely acknowledged, but it is for his close friendships with and support for the ordinary working people of the country that he should be best remembered. Despite never being in the Cabinet he was without doubt a notable political figure of the period. He had a close but difficult working relationship with Gladstone and was on friendly terms with Disraeli; he seems to have enjoyed a special friendship with Queen Victoria whom he met often at Privy Council meetings and occasional social events; and his passing was mourned throughout the country. According to reports, as soon as the news reached Salisbury, all the shops were closed and a great crowd gathered silently in the market place to express the grief of the people of this city.

The news spread through the city with extraordinary rapidity. Groups assembled at the street corners asking if it could be true. Only a week ago Professor Fawcett was seen in the city, his tall form attracting the attention of every passer-by. A month since he was a member of a pleasant picnic party at Mr Councillor Lovibond's.

The Marquis of Hartington announced his death to a packed and hushed House of Commons and almost broke down as he spoke. The following day Prime Minister Gladstone paid tribute to him.

Henry was buried at Trumpington, a small village just outside Cambridge. Salisbury had been considered but Millicent decided that the strain of a large and very public funeral would be too great for his elderly parents. In the event she was proved right as many thousands of people descended on Trumpington to pay their respects. In addition to the statue in Salisbury's market place, a number of other memorials to Henry Fawcett were erected. There are three in London including the national memorial in St George's Chapel in Westminster Abbey dedicated to both Henry and Millicent.

Perhaps the extraordinary affection in which Henry Fawcett was held by all classes of society in this country is best illustrated by two of the hundreds of letters Millicent received following her husband's death :

'Balmoral Castle, November 8, 1884.
DEAR MRS. FAWCETT, I am anxious to express to you myself the true and sincere sympathy I feel for you in your present terrible bereavement, as well as my sincere regret for the loss of your distinguished husband, who bore his great trial with such courage and patience, and who served his Queen and country ably and faithfully.

You, who were so devoted a wife to him, must, even in this hour of overwhelming grief, be gratified by the universal expression of respect and regret on this sad occasion.

That He who alone can give consolation and peace in the hour of affliction may support you, is the earnest wish of yours sincerely.
[Signed]   VICTORIA, R. AND I.'

'PANGBOURNE, November 8, 1884.
DEAR MADAM, I hope you will forgive us, but having followed the political life of the late Professor Fawcett, we felt when we saw his death in the papers on the 7th that we had lost a personal friend, and that a great man had gone from us. The loss to you must be beyond measure; but we as part of the nation do give you who have been his helper our heartfelt sympathy in your great trouble, and we do hope you may find a little consolation in knowing that his work that he has done for the working classes has not been in vain.

We, as working men, do offer you and your child our deepest sympathy, and beg to be yours respectfully,

HARRY COX, CHARLES EDDY, RICHARD BOWLES, WILLIAM COX
(Carpenters)

G. LEWENDON, GEORGE BROWN (Bricklayers)

CHARLES COX (Blacksmith)

M. CLIFFORD (Postmaster)

F. CLIFFORD   (Clerk)

Fine obituaries for a great Salisbury man.

Bibliographical Note

There is no modern biography of Henry Fawcett. His friend Leslie Stephen wrote *The Life of Henry Fawcett*, published in 1885, very shortly after his death. The other main source for this paper is *A Beacon for the Blind* by Winifred Holt, first published 1915. Millicent Fawcett's autobiography *What I Remember* (1924) records a great deal about their life together, but says very little about his death. The biography of Millicent by Ray Strachey (1931) is another valuable source, as is Elizabeth Crawford's latest book *Enterprising Women: The Garretts and their Circle* (2002).

Peter Fawcett's father, Sidney Fawcett, wrote an article in an early issue of *The Hatcher Review* which has been reprinted in *Salisbury Spectrum* (1984, 1996) entitled 'The Statue in the Market Place' which includes a brief description of the unveiling of the statue. In Salisbury Museum Library there is a volume of newspaper cuttings relating to Henry Fawcett, including obituaries from all over the country, and reviews of Stephen's book.

Community Policing in Late Medieval Salisbury:

The Role of the Urban Coroner

Carrie Smith

T he discussion which follows has arisen partly out of irritation with the way in which politicians and the popular press persist in using the term 'medieval' to describe behaviour, values, opinions, morals and, in particular, administrations and legal and penal systems which they wish to decry. As a consequence 'medieval' has become a pejorative term, to be interpreted as meaning unfair, cruel, inefficient, corrupt, barbaric, and politically to the right of Genghis Khan.

Historians must bear some of the blame for this, particularly those of us whose interest lies in investigating the workings and efficiency or otherwise of the medieval criminal justice system and the maintenance of law and order in medieval society. Our studies have undeniably laid bare certain truths. One is that the punishments prescribed under medieval law were severe and inflexible. Even for minor offences like petty theft they usually resulted in instant and permanent physical disfigurement. Never again could that man or woman pass as an upright member of society. For a felony – and we should remember that most offences were classed as felonies – the punishment was death, usually by hanging, sometimes by burning, and in some places by more bizarre and arcane methods.[1] A second is that law enforcement, which depended on unpaid, largely unsupervised, locally prominent individuals appointed, often doubtless through influence, to official positions, was not efficient in bringing offenders to justice. This applied particularly in rural areas or when suspected offenders were of high social status. Thirdly, conviction rates of the few who were brought to trial were low. So perhaps it is unsurprising that the perception has grown that England in the later Middle Ages was a lawless place in which life was cheap, violence was rampant, and the king's justice was daily subverted and abused not only by those with access to power, patronage, and wealth, but by the very people whose business it should have been to implement it impartially.

A re-evaluation of these perceptions is surely called for. They are too generalized. It is possible, where surviving records allow, to examine the functioning of the law and its officials in the context of specific communities, particularly with regard to the actions taken when a homicide occurred, and to reach rather different conclusions. This brief study will focus on responses to homicide in Salisbury in the later fourteenth century.

A bustling and prosperous town whose population in 1377 was probably close to 5,000 people,[2] Salisbury was largely self-governing. It had a mayor, four aldermen, two reeves, and two coroners, and a prison regularly delivered by royal justices.[3] While most of its officials were subordinate to those of the bishop of Salisbury, to whom the town belonged, its coroners, being royal officials, were not.[4] The coroners of Salisbury were men familiar with the responsibilities of office and intimately connected with their town's mercantile and political fortunes. A few examples will suffice. Robert Bont, Richard Jewell, Richard Spencer, and William Warmwell all represented the city in parliament, often more than once.[5] Spencer, Warmwell, and Jewell were also among those who in 1395 represented the city in a dispute with the bishop over tallage [a tax] and were named in the loyal address from Salisbury's citizens to Richard II in 1399.[6] In 1412 Spencer was named as one of the feoffees for property given to the town and was paid expenses for conducting business on the town's behalf in London.[7] Warmwell and in all likelihood Bont were each mayor twice, and Geoffrey de Warminster and John Upton were mayor once.[8] The family of William Godmanstone, alderman of Meadow ward in the 1370s, had two chantry chaplains in St Thomas's church in the late 14th century.[9] Warminster owned an inn called 'Countewelle's' in the High Street.[10] Warmwell contributed £20 towards the purchase of the George Inn for the town in 1404, and by his will devised property to the mayor and commonalty of the town and gave a silver chalice to St. Thomas's church.[11] Most were probably of the mercantile and property-owning elite; Spencer and Warmwell, for example, are known to have dealt in cloth, while Bont's family had property both inside and outside the town.[12]

These intimate connections between Salisbury and the men who served as its coroners gave those officials several immediate advantages over their colleagues who operated in rural areas. It is clear from the amount of detail given in surviving Salisbury inquests that bodies were examined quickly, before decomposition blurred or obliterated marks of violence; eye-witnesses, plentiful in the crowded urban environment even at night, were questioned before memories faded or became corrupted, and there was little time for interested parties to concoct a plausible story founded on rumour or outright untruth. Those suspected of or indicted for a homicide found it harder to escape arrest. Well-known to their fellow citizens and trusted by them to act in the city's interests, Salisbury coroners could expect co-operation and assistance. Rural coroners on the other hand were outsiders, little known to most of the communities where they were called on to act and who, since their presence was always attended by inconvenience and expense, often experienced difficulties in empanelling juries and were doubtless frequently lied to.[13]

In the 32 surviving coroners' inquests into homicides in Salisbury between the 1360s and the mid 1380s 33 suspects were named. Three, one of whom is known to have abjured [agreed to banishment from the kingdom], took sanctuary in churches, and of the six who escaped three did so at night, when darkness made flight easier. Seventeen – slightly over 50% – were arrested. By comparison with contemporary rural arrests for homicide this is a remarkably high figure. Of those arrested, it has been possible to trace the trial outcomes of eight, and some of these are discussed below. In six cases named suspects were apparently not detained. Four of these cases will now be considered in more detail since they have a direct bearing on the second part of my argument – that despite the very clear demands of the law, community consensus, with the active collusion of the coroners, was adept at manipulating judicial outcomes into conformity with popular opinion if the penalty demanded by the law was deemed to be inappropriate in particular circumstances.

The first case concerns the death of William Devenays. The inquest jurors said that he and his brother Henry had set upon their other brother John with swords and knocked him to the ground. John's son John then intervened, stood over his father's prostrate form, and pleaded with his uncles to stop. They turned their swords on him instead and wounded him, whereupon he stabbed his uncle William in the stomach with a dagger. The jurors had a clear legal requirement to indict John, who should then have been arrested, and who could at his trial have pleaded self-defence. Instead, they stated quite specifically that no one was guilty of William's death. In law, this statement was patently false. The emphasis placed in the narrative on the fact that John was acting to protect his apparently defenceless father, that John's uncles initiated the attack, and that only after John's attempts at mediation had failed and he himself had been wounded did he respond to the assault clearly demonstrates the consensus of community opinion, which was that William had got his just desserts. Other factors may also have contributed. John's uncles had swords, vastly more dangerous weapons than John's knife, and William survived long enough to receive the last rites. As part of that ritual he would have been encouraged not only to repent his own sins but to forgive those who had sinned against him. The importance of the fact that he did not die unshriven must be stressed; in the medieval belief system, the soul was more important than the body. Nevertheless, the jurors clearly overstepped or ignored their legal obligations. However strongly they might slant their narrative to give John the best possible case for obtaining an acquittal or permission to apply for a pardon, they had no right to refuse to indict him at all and certainly none to declare that the death was no one's fault.

An identical verdict was recorded in the death of Richard Clere. He and his wife Margaret had argued with William Polemond at John Cook's house. Richard, who according to the jurors 'had a terrible name for homicide and was reputed to be dangerous', threatened to harm William the following day and then, with Margaret, left the house. The couple hid outside and lay in wait for William who, understandably terrified, remained in the house for a considerable time. When he eventually left it was dark and he did not see the lurking couple, but a neighbour who apparently had seen them hide and was obviously awaiting developments with interest shouted a loud warning and William tried to run away. Having lost the advantage of surprise, Richard tried to detain him by entangling him with his cloak, whereupon William in panic stabbed Richard in the arm. Once again the jurors specifically stated that no one was guilty of the death. Here, too, obvious mitigating factors have been incorporated into the jurors' narrative; a premeditated attack by a well-known local thug under cover of darkness, and the infliction in self-defence, by a man in fear of his life, of a relatively minor wound which was not immediately fatal – Richard did not die until ten days later, presumably as a result of infection, and received the last rites. Nevertheless William should have been indicted, arrested, and tried, but once again the jurors baldly ignored correct legal procedure. (In fact, William very sensibly took the precaution of obtaining a pardon, which he produced to the judges of King's Bench when they sat as justices in the town in 1384.)

Similar strategies to avoid apportioning blame can be seen in other cases where the jurors avoided making any statement at all indicating their verdict. John Mayn, for example, attempted to break up a fight between Thomas Lollow and John Laurence. He wrapped his cloak round his hand and tried to grab Thomas's knife, but his hand was badly cut and he died 12 days later. Since John's death did not result immediately from the wound some kind of infection may be presumed. He too received the last rites. Although Thomas had apparently not intended to cause John any harm, he should have been indicted and arrested; when the case came to trial both he and the community could confidently have expected either an acquittal, a verdict of accidental death, or permission to apply for a pardon. Instead, the lack of any statement from the jurors linking Thomas with the death, and of any mention of whether he was arrested or fled, suggests that no action was taken to detain him. As a final example there is the case of Walter Hanle, a king's serjeant-at-arms. The jurors stated that Richard Perot had assaulted him at the New Inn with a knife and a sword. They described (I am tempted to say with admiration) the rather dashing sleight of hand with which Walter used his cloak to entrap Richard's sword against his chest and then, with the little knife hanging at his right side, struck Richard in the left arm. The narrative stacks up the odds in Walter's favour; he had overcome, by ingenuity and with only one small weapon, an assailant with two, one of which was a larger and more dangerous one, and apparently inflicted only the minimum injury necessary to end the attack. The jurors clearly stated that in no other way could Walter have escaped death, and once again the dead man had languished for more than a fortnight and received the last rites. While one should not discount Walter's official position and status as factors in the jurors' failure to name him as responsible for the death and in the community's failure to detain him for trial, Walter too could have expected a verdict of self-defence or permission to apply for a pardon.

Prisoners held on remand had their cases heard before justices at courts known as gaol deliveries. If the trial outcomes of the eight men whose cases can be followed in gaol delivery records are reviewed, we find that one was acquitted altogether,[14] one was found to have acted in self-defence,[15] four were remanded to await pardon,[16] and only two were hanged. In the first of those two cases, Roger Sporiere is said to have been attacked in his own house by a man called Richard Essex, who stabbed him in the arm with a knife. Roger died as a result of his wound 11 days later.[17] In the second, Walter Panchener was alleged to have assaulted Walter Ford and stabbed him in the heart with a knife. Walter died immediately.[18] Juries at gaol delivery had a strong local component and in Salisbury almost certainly included men who had participated in the original inquest; one must therefore conclude that by bringing in trial verdicts which sent these two men to their deaths they were reflecting public opinion that these two particular homicides deserved to be dealt with severely. In the first of these cases, this may have been partly due to the fact that the victim was attacked in his own home. Not for nothing is the Englishman's house said to be his castle. And in a period when surnames were not fixed, Essex's name may reflect his geographical origin; if so, as an outsider to the local community he had less claim to its compassion than a resident of the town. Significant factors in the other case may be that Walter was stabbed in the chest, a wound obviously intended to cause death rather than to maim or disable, and that he consequently died unshriven, his soul despatched to purgatory without any priestly intercession to assist in shortening its stay there.

Naturally one must be cautious when dealing with the narratives found in homicide inquests and trials. Even in the Salisbury coroners' inquests, whose narratives are vastly more detailed and likely to contain a greater proportion of truth than those of rural coroners, it is always necessary to bear in mind that one cannot know what information the jurors excluded and that there were many factors which influenced what information they did give and how it was presented. There is always the possibility that sometimes they simply lied. The popularity and personality of both victim and suspect, as well as any history of offending or violent behaviour by either, were doubtless among the factors which inclined the community, as represented by the jury, to obtain a particular outcome. It should be remembered that at Salisbury coroners' inquests those whose presence was compulsory included not only the jurymen and the first finder of the body and his or her pledges, but the aldermen and four residents of each of the four wards. At least 35 individuals were therefore present; there were also unknown numbers of witnesses, other local officials including those with custody of any arrested suspect, relatives and friends of both victim and suspect, and of course the simply curious, of whom no doubt there were many. Coroners' inquests were therefore gatherings which in a very real sense represented the whole urban community. Whether what the jurors said was true or not is in fact largely irrelevant; the point is that the stories they told represented their view of the relative roles both victims and culprits had played in the incidents, the amount of blame attached to each, and, by implication, what action, if any, should be taken in the matter. It should also be remembered that when King's Bench justices visited the regions, they could and did fine officials and communities who brought in false verdicts, overstepped their jurisdictions, or failed to pursue suspected criminals. However infrequent their visitations might be, the willingness of Salisbury's urban community to risk incurring such costs is strong additional evidence of the townspeople's determination to ensure that the law was applied as they deemed appropriate.

From the examples cited here one can see that local communities could and did manipulate the law in order to achieve outcomes they considered to be fair and equitable – what might be described as popular justice. It has long been known that trial juries did so. By failing to turn up for the trial at the first gaol delivery session a suspected offender would continue to be held in the unpleasant and life-threatening conditions prevalent in a medieval gaol; if he or she survived until a subsequent session, that same jury would acquit. The jurors were thereby converting a prison from its ostensible purpose, which was only to hold prisoners until trial, into a punishment which the community they represented hoped would deter further bad or criminal behaviour. Simul-taneously, they avoided inflicting a punishment they felt to be inappropriately severe.[19] It is not unreasonable to suggest that urban coroners similarly viewed their role at least partially as that of mediating between the requirements of the law and the opinion of the community – which, it must be remembered, included relatives and friends of both victim and culprit. Thus they actively colluded with the community to ensure that where law and community consensus conflicted the outcome of any homicide inquest was that demanded by local public opinion rather that required by a strict application of the law.

In any densely populated urban environment, whether historical or modern, law enforcement can only function effectively by consent. Urban coroners had to perform a delicate balancing act. On the one hand, if they did not fulfil their official obligations adequately the king might revoke the town's privilege of electing its own coroners. That privilege not only marked its status but preserved its citizens from interference by outsiders. On the other hand, as townsmen living within the community they served, coroners needed the respect and confidence of that community in order to maintain their own status and mercantile success. They dared not antagonise or outrage the very people who traded with them and who elected them to parliament and to posts within the urban administration. Urban coroners were uniquely placed to enforce the law more effectively than their counterparts working in rural areas, and to do so in a manner acceptable to and supported by the local community. When homicides occurred, urban coroners and their fellow townspeople acted together to achieve pragmatic outcomes which were acceptable to public opinion and reflected fine nuances of guilt and blame which the blunt instrument of the law could not accommodate.

Inefficiency, corruption, and injustice are failings common to legal and judicial systems in all times and places. Of course the failings and inadequacies of the medieval legal system rightly need to be explored and discussed. But one must not ignore the occasions when, even if it did not function exactly as intended, it nevertheless worked, worked well, and worked to the benefit of medieval society. 'Medieval' is, after all, an adjective describing a period of history. It is not, and should never be used as, an insult.

Notes

1   Thorne, S E (ed) (1977) *Bracton: On the Laws and Customs of England.* London: Selden Society., *passim*; Bateson, Mary (ed) (1904, 1906) *Borough Customs* (Selden Society vols 18, 21), *passim*.
2   Crittall, Elizabeth (1962) *Victoria History of Wiltshire* vol 6. London: Oxford Univ. Press., 72, 94.
3   *ibid.*, 94–5, 96, 99.
4   *ibid.*, 99.
5   *ibid.*, 104.
6   Carr, David R (2001) *The First General Entry Book of the City of Salisbury, 1387–1452* (Wiltshire Record Society vol 54), 63.
7   *ibid.*, 49.
8   Crittall 1962, 95, 99n, 103.
9   e.g. PRO, JUST 2/199, rott. 3, 4; Crittall 1962, 148, 150.
10 Crittall, 1962, 81.
11 Carr 2001, 20; Crittall 1962, 151.
12 Crittall 1962, 125, 126, 104.
13 Hunnisett, Roy F (1961) *The Medieval Coroner.* Cambridge: Cambridge Univ. Press, 127.
14 PRO, JUST 3/156, rot. 4.
15 *ibid.*, JUST 3/161, rot. 18.
16 *ibid.*, C 160/183; JUST 3/151, rot. 1; JUST 3/156, rott. 9d., 14; JUST 3/161, rot. 18.
17 *ibid.*, JUST 3/151, rot. 1.
18 *ibid.*, JUST 3/156, rot. 14.
19 Ireland, Richard W (1987) 'Theory and Practice within the Medieval English Prison'. *American Journal of Legal History* vol. 31, 56–67.

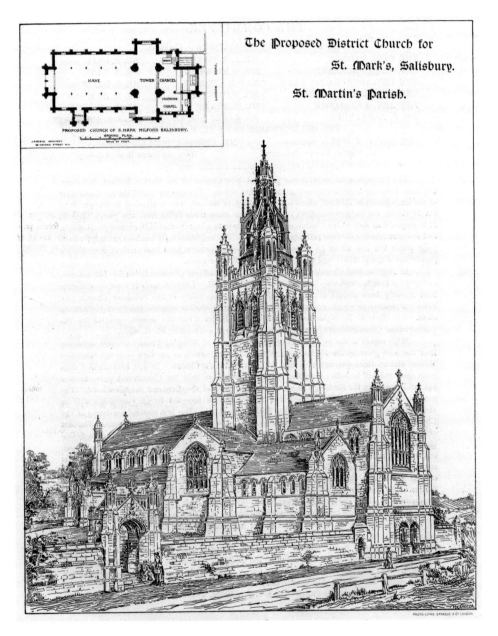

St Mark's appeal leaflet with engraving of the proposed design by J A Reeve.

J Arthur Reeve and St Mark's Church, Salisbury

Peter Barrie

The casual visitor to Salisbury, approaching the city by the ring road, would find it difficult to avoid a large towerless late Victorian church looking rather lost, and forlornly presiding over an ugly roundabout constructed in the 1960s. Despite its rather forbidding initial appearance and unprepossessing surroundings, St Mark's Church has a most interesting history, and its largely forgotten architect, Joseph Arthur Reeve (1850-1915), was linked to William Burges and some of his greatest clients. Reeve's fortuitous family connections put him into contact with Archbishop Benson and Bishop John Wordsworth, and both men provided him with a number of prestigious commissions, including the most important of his career – St Mark's Church. This is his story.

Joseph Arthur Reeve was born in 1850, son of Rev Andrewes Reeve, the incumbent of Kimmeridge church, Dorset from 1853 to 1862. Due to his father's career, he was exposed to church architecture from an early age. After finishing his education in Exeter, Reeve was first articled to the architect E J Tarver (1841-1891)[1] who himself first worked for Benjamin Ferrey from 1858-62.[2] Tarver, after 'obtaining various prizes at the Architectural Association, commenced work on his own account in 1863',[3] and was proposed to the RIBA in 1865 by his employer Ferrey, plus T Roger Smith and William Burges. Tarver's association with Burges continued in 1869 when he and Horatio Walter Lonsdale were employed as draftsmen on his book of *Architectural Drawings*, but this work was somewhat pre-empted by the publication of Viollet le-Duc's *Dictionnaire*.[4] Joe Mordaunt Crook describes both men as protégés of Burges.

In view of Tarver's employment with Burges, it is no surprise that Reeve later found employment with him after serving his articles,[5] doubtless through his former employer's recommendation. Burges did not have a large architectural office,[6] so in all likelihood the two men would have worked closely together.

Burges was in an unusual position for a 19th-century architect in that he was independently wealthy, and could therefore choose commissions he considered sufficiently interesting. He also had the fabulously wealthy Lord Bute as a patron.[7] Consequently, Reeve's early career with Burges must have im-pressed upon the young man the importance of patronage if he was to succeed.

The fact that Reeve was to enjoy success professionally in his chosen path in later life had much to do with the close friendship between Dr Edward White Benson and his brother, the Rev John Andrewes Reeve. Benson was a Headmaster of Wellington College, Chancellor of Lincoln Cathedral, the first Bishop of Truro, and later Archbishop of Canterbury. John Reeve first met Benson while serving at St Mary's, Nottingham, and was summoned to be one of his examining Chaplains at Wellington.[8] The two men struck up a close friendship, and when Benson was appointed Bishop of Truro in 1877, he asked Reeve to come too and take up a post as Curate of Kenwyn Church. He later wrote him a long letter entreating him not to go to India to do missionary work.[9] Benson's rise to power was rapid and after supervising J L Pearson's building of the new Cathedral at Truro, he was appointed Archbishop of Canterbury in 1882. However, Benson ensured that his friend John was near, prompting him to write:

> I never realised till he asked me to be Vicar of Addington [where the Archbishop's Palace was situated] how much I longed to be near him; and the happiness of being with him first in his country home, and afterwards at Lambeth, [Benson appointed him Rector there as well – the building is next to Lambeth Palace] has been to me a fresh and joyful inspiration.[10]

One act that was to have had a profound effect on J A Reeve's career was the marriage in 1874 of his sister Mary to Rev Christopher Wordsworth, the noted Cambridge scholar,[11] son of Bishop Christopher Wordsworth of Lincoln,[12] and brother of Bishop John Wordsworth of Salisbury.

For J A Reeve, a London architect with a small practice, a filial connection with a notable clerical dynasty was fortuitous to say the least. Both his brother-in-law Christopher and Bishop John Wordsworth were to grant their patronage to him very liberally. The first commission Bishop Wordsworth entrusted to Reeve was to carry out alterations to the Bishop's Palace in Salisbury. The fact that plans relating to suggested alterations are dated May 1889, so soon after Wordsworth took up his new appointment in 1885, indicate his keenness to restore the Palace and improve amenities. According to the plans, Reeve's work consisted mostly of rearranging a back staircase and creating a new passageway to the drawing room, although new exterior doors and window-dressings were also shown.[13] By his own admission, Reeve's restoration of the palace was not entirely a repair of the existing fabric of the undercroft – it also had an element of conjecture about it:

> Of this thirteenth century work the undercroft beneath the great hall or 'aula'
> remains intact, although as now restored it does not present exactly the same
> appearance as it did originally . . . The side windows of the undercroft were also
> rather different in Bishop Poore's design from what they now appear, for the
> detached columns supporting the inner arches in the centre have been inserted
> to give greater lightness to the general effect of the room . . . The size and form of
> the lights themselves must be very nearly the same as Bishop Poore's design, and
> enough of the inner arches remain when the restoration was taken in hand to
> make it possible to reproduce them exactly.[14]

The 1993 Royal Commission publication on the Bishop's Palace states
that Reeve 'removed an inserted partition considered to be medieval, which
divided off the two S bays of the undercroft'.[15] Reeve does not mention this,
only commenting that 'With regard to the date of the wall which now divides the
undercroft into two parts, leaving two bays to the north and one to the south, it
is difficult to speak with certainty, but there can be no question that it is an
ancient erection.'[16] Reeve himself did not give any justification for inserting new
work in the windows and removing the partition, but the *Episcopal Palaces of
England*, published five years after Reeve's restoration, provides a useful
contemporary commentary on the work done on the undercroft:

> This noble apartment, degraded and defaced, and cut up by modern partitions
> into domestic offices, has been restored by the present Bishop, and exhibits an
> admirable specimen of the domestic architecture of the time of Henry III. With
> some necessary modifications of the windows to admit more light, while still
> preserving their old design, it forms a stately servants' hall.[17]

Following the restoration, Bishop Wordsworth was obviously feeling
sufficiently knowledgeable about the history of his residence to give a lecture at
the Blackmore Museum, Salisbury on 27 January 1890. This was entitled 'The
Bishop's Palace of Salisbury' in which he refers to 'the vaulted room and
passage that I have just had the pleasure of restoring with the kind advice and
oversight of Mr Arthur Reeve.'[18] Reeve obviously shared his patron's pleasure
because he followed Wordsworth's lecture with one of his own called 'Notes on
the Architectural History of the Palace.'[19]

Bishop Wordsworth installed his brother as Master of St Nicholas'
Hospital, an ancient almshouse in Salisbury, and a building that dates from
approximately the same time as the cathedral. Christopher seems to have had
the same enthusiasm for restoration as his brother, and after his appointment
instituted repairs. While Reeve was employed by Burges, William Butterfield
had been employed to carry out work on the chapel and almshouses,[20] and to
this Reeve added a covered walkway to protect the residents from inclement
weather.[21] He also designed a pair of altar lights.

Illustration by Reeve from The Fifteenth Century Cartulary of St Nicholas Hospital, Salisbury with other records *edited by Rev Christopher Wordsworth.*

Before the most important commission of Reeve's career, St Mark's Church, he carried out the restoration of Ramsbury Church. The first reference to this work in the *Salisbury Diocesan Gazette*, 1890, states that:

> This ancient and interesting structure, standing on the site of the original Cathedral of the Diocese [The church was built on an early Minster site which was the Bishop's seat in the tenth and eleventh centuries] containing much thirteenth century, if not earlier work, is about to be restored to its original beauty . . . The Bishop has called a meeting of the Churchmen of the Diocese, to assemble, . . . at the Town Hall, Marlborough, on Thursday May 1 . . . The Bishop will ask the meeting to appoint a committee, representing the whole Diocese, to undertake this great and important work.[22]

The patroness was Baroness Angela Burdett Coutts who contributed £1,000 to the restoration.[23] The *Salisbury Diocesan Gazette* went on to say that 'A report upon the church has been received by Mr J Arthur Reeve, of London at the request of the Baroness Burdett Coutts.[24]

There does not appear to be any other connection between Reeve and Burdett Coutts, so the likelihood is that Wordsworth recommended him for the task on the strength of his work at the Bishop's Palace. However, Reeve did carry out painted decoration in St Stephen's, Westminster by Benjamin Ferrey, the church Burdett Coutts had paid for.[25] At Ramsbury Reeve removed galleries at the west end 'being of an unsightly character', removed the pulpit with sounding board and put the replacement pulpit 'in memory of the late Vicar'[26] on the opposite side of the chancel arch, moved the font, removed the box pews, replaced the old porch, and made general repairs to the church.[27]

The decision to commission a new parish church for the ancient cathedral city of Salisbury[28] was the momentous and fulfilled vision of the Bishop of the Diocese, John Wordsworth. The Wyndham Park area of Salisbury had been extensively developed from the late 19th century as a consequence of it being sold by Dr Bourne in 1871, and the ground laid out into residential streets. In view of this Wordsworth considered that steps had to be taken to tend to the spiritual needs of the local populace. In 1879 a temporary iron church was erected under the control of Rev C N Wyld, the Rector of St Martin's Church, in which parish the new structure was to be situated, but nothing was done towards building a more permanent structure. His Curate, Rev Sydney Dugdale, ministered to the people there, but Bishop Wordsworth had rather grander plans for the area, and decided that the time had come for a building more worthy of its status to be erected.[29]

On 19 September 1890, the Bishop wrote to Rev Dugdale stressing that plans for a new parish church should commence, and that he would be willing to contribute £500 towards it. However, he had a number of conditions: that he should be on the building committee, that Sir Arthur Blomfield should be judge of an architectural competition because he was 'consulting architect of the Cathedral, and stood almost at the head of his profession,'[30] and that Wordsworth should have the option to nominate two architects to take part. In his first letter to Rev Dugdale regarding the new church, Blomfield advised that

> I should say that five or six Architects if carefully chosen would be quite enough. You are not likely I think to get any well known Church Architect to compete, but there are plenty of young men now, who are quite capable of designing a good Church and who, having little to do, would be glad to do it.[31]

On 15 October 1890 the Bishop met the Mayor and local dignitaries, and proposed that the 'Weeping Cross' site that the Ecclesiastical Commissioners had offered be accepted, and that J A Reeve, George Gordon, C E Ponting, M Harding and F Bath be asked to submit designs for the new church. In addition, J T Micklethwaite was also invited to compete and commented that 'I should much like to design the church, but it has not been our custom to engage in competitions which seldom end satisfactorily to any of the parties concerned'.[32] He also suggested that 'the committee follow the example of the Liverpool Cathedral committee and invite those which they select to submit drawings of works already done and let Sir Arthur choose from them'. Harding declined to submit a design on the grounds that he had too much work in hand, and had a connection with St Mark's.[33]

The conditions of the competition were rigorous, firstly specifying that the cost of the building (excepting the tower) was not to exceed £5,000. In

1890 this was not a large sum of money to spend on a church 160 ft long, and by way of comparison, Butterfield's flagship, All Saints Margaret Street in London, started in 1850, was approximately 100 ft in length and cost £70,000![34] The brief to architects went on to state that 'The committee suggest that brick should not be the material employed, and that the style should be the late pointed.'[35] This would appear to be a conscious decision by the committee to rule out the possibility of any entries resembling a polychromatic brick structure in the manner of Street or Butterfield. They must have decided amongst themselves that this was a real danger, and that it was as well to make their intentions clear.

The instructions to architects clearly pointed to a very English structure, so Wordsworth and his committee would have been aware of current architectural trends in their desire for a church built in the indigenous Perpendicular style. The adjudicator, Sir Arthur Blomfield, who designed St Mary Portsea (1887-9) as a great perpendicular town church, also had influence in the matter; this is confirmed in a letter to Dugdale in which he stated 'I have not the least doubt that your draft of conditions to architects embodies everything I could suggest.'[36]

The competing architects were instructed to submit designs anonymously on Blomfield's advice, who stated that, 'to avoid any suspicion of partiality it would be as well for all designs to be distinguished by a device or motto.'[37] This may have been a precaution to protect Wordsworth from criticism, as by this date he was actively and publicly associated with Reeve due to the Bishop's Palace lectures they both gave. This is intimated in a letter from Dugdale to Blomfield in which he stated that: 'We have had some difficulty in deciding what architect to employ; various gentlemen being favoured by different persons in the Parish.'[38] No specific evidence exists to suggest who favoured which architect, but one of Blomfield's conditions was that, on becoming assessor of the competition, he should have the last word on the winner:

> If I am asked by the committee to act as Assessor in the Competition to which you refer, I shall be willing to do so if they will agree to act on my recommendation, if I should report any one design (complying with the conditions laid down) to be distinctly the best.[39]

On 5 February Blomfield sent Dugdale his report on the five designs submitted, and commented that 'I think that for many reasons it is better not to enter, in writing, into criticisms of the various plans, more especially as I know that the decision at which I have arrived is in accordance with the opinion already formed by the committee.'[40] Blomfield stated that the winning design was 'Anglicanus', but that the two runners up had been 'evidently prepared with much care and thought, and in some respects shew considerable power and originality.'[41] Unfortunately no reference in the St Mark's archive exists to indicate who the authors of 'Nisi Dominus' and 'Line for Line' were, so we must accept Blomfield's judgment in the matter. He went on to state that 'I find that there is some inaccuracy in calculating the number of sittings' with the winning design, but it was decided that this could be modified under his guidance.[42]

More complications ensued when Blomfield wrote privately to Dugdale saying that 'The point raised by the non-compliance of "Anglicanus" with the precise letter of the instructions to Architects, is one which may, I think, be laid hold of by the other Competitors.'[43] This referred to sending a quote from a 'First rate firm of builders', stating that they would complete the church for £5,300, instead of sending in his own estimate of costs. The problem arose because according to the conditions the cost was to be 'not exceeding £5000.'[44] Blomfield wrote that 'my view is, that though he has not complied with the letter he has in no way violated the spirit of those instructions.'[45] At this point Blomfield sought the opinion of Ewan Christian, Consulting Architect of the Ecclesiastical Commissioners, stating that he was someone 'who has had as large an experience as anyone in judging competitions', to ascertain if the winning architect was ineligible after this infringement. He replied 'I think not'.[46]

Reeve acknowledged the news that he had won the competition with what would appear to be surprise, and stated that 'You can imagine that I am intensely delighted at the result of the competition. I never dared to hope for success.'[47] When the committee accepted Reeve's design for St Mark's, the other competing architects gave a varied response to the news. The first to acknowledge his fee for entering the competition was Micklethwaite, who philosophically commented, 'I see that fortune is against us this time.'[48] In marked contrast, Fred Bath complained that 'I fully expected that the committee would have adopted the usual and commendable custom of exhibiting drawings and reports, which personally I should much like to be done.'[49] Bath was not the only aggrieved party and when Reeve thought he would be expected to have the foundations dug out at his own risk, he wrote that, 'I have never competed [in an architectural competition] before and I never will again unless the conditions are of a very different nature and less distinctly antagonistic to the successful competitor'.[50] Blomfield managed to persuade the committee and wrote, 'I strongly advise the committee not to abandon his design';[51] this counsel was acted upon.

Despite the fact that he had experience of church restoration, by the time he won the St Mark's competition, Reeve's only other experience of designing a church was his St Anne's, Roath, which was partly opened in 1887. This commission had a smaller accommodation requirement, but the floor plans of the two buildings are remarkably similar, both having wide chancels without a

*St Anne's, Roath, Cardiff (*The Builder *November 5 1887)*

screen, and a baptistery occupying the same position. Other similarities included a Morning Chapel from which communicants could leave the high altar, identical tiling on the floors, and a similar intended treatment of the roofs. St Anne's was Reeve's first opportunity to test his ideas about church building and were to be put into practice at St Mark's five years later.

Reeve's patron, Bishop Wordsworth, had wanted his architect to design a building that would be 'worthy to rank beside the beautiful churches of the older Salisbury parishes,'[52] and it was reported that, 'The style of the church throughout is late 15th century, and that 'The tracery of the windows has been varied so that no two are alike.[53] Now that Reeve's design had been adopted, the building committee accepted Hayes of Bristol's tender, and Wordsworth instructed Reeve to have the building started in October 1891.[54] The foundation stone was laid by Archbishop Benson on 27 April 1892, [55] though limited funds were to cause problems, obliging them to construct chancel, vestries, morning chapel and transepts piecemeal, and Reeve warned that 'the more a building is split into small sections the more expensive it must become.'[56]

Later in 1892 more problems ensued when Reeve discovered that the committee wanted the side chapel added, which he said was:

A useless addition to the church and in as much as it splits up into one or more subdivisions it assuredly represents extra expense; – the whole question strikes me thus, either the church is wanted or it is not wanted, if the latter why was it ever started if the former I am absolutely certain it is short sighted policy on the part of the committee to take the line that they have done up to the present time, make a really good start and let the church take a fairly prominent position in the place and I feel certain that people will come forward to help, but to erect a small fragment as proposed, is I am certain dangerous . . . I write this to you as a friend, not in my capacity of architect to the committee.[57]

However, the advice was ignored and the chapel duly added. The church continued to be built in sections throughout 1893, and was 'very decently done notwithstanding the constant want of supervision.'[58] Wordsworth dedicated the finished portion of the church on 28 April 1894, though St Mark's had to wait until 1915 before the nave was dedicated.

Reeve had originally intended for a grand west porch, but this was abandoned along with vaulting for the crossing, west gallery and baptistery, carving at the entrance to the gallery staircase and the exterior of the south aisle. Reeve also prepared a design for a south porch (executed posthumously), but it bears

St Mark's, Salisbury - laying of the foundation stone by Archbishop Benson on
27 April 1892.

a very striking resemblance to his porch at Ramsbury, suggesting economy of design as well as finance!

Like many 19th-century Gothic Revival architects, Reeve was very versatile, and besides churches, he also designed a 'vast amount of church furniture, all of which shows careful thought and refinement of detail, and at St Mark's his designs included the high altar (constructed to be seen with and

Altar Cloth designed by J A Reeve for the Private Chapel of Lambeth Palace (The Builder 7 November 1885)

without frontals), a credence table, readers' desk and choir stalls.[59] His needlework design for the St Mark's processional banner, depicting the patron of the building, still exists in the church, and this makes an interesting contrast to the altar frontal which Benson commisisioned him to design for the private chapel at Lambeth Palace in 1885.[60]

Despite the fact that Reeve 'took a keen interest in colour decoration,'[61] and had decorated interiors of a number of London churches,[62] he did not venture to design glass himself. In 1898 he commissioned his old acquaintance Lonsdale to design a series of windows for the Lady Chapel of St Mark's. They comprised an east window depicting the Blessed Virgin Mary flanked by St Ursula and Mary Magdalene, and for the south windows, St Mark, St Paul, Claudia, Lois and Eunice, three women from the New Testament.

Reeve also completed a very personal commission for Bishop Wordsworth, a 'beautiful pastoral staff in sculptured ivory enriched with jewels,'[63] which was presented by Canon Charles Myers on 27 October 1909 'to be used by the Bishops of Salisbury within the Cathedral.'[64] This seems to have been a speciality of Reeve's, and he also designed staffs for the Bishops of Edinburgh and Norwich.[65] Wordsworth's biography also records that 'In St Mark's Church, Salisbury, consecrated by him, a small standing effigy has been erected, designed by Mr Arthur Reeve, facing that of St Osmund.'[66] Wordsworth died suddenly in 1911, and his body was laid to rest under a memorial cross designed by Reeve at Britford Church near Salisbury.

Unfortunately Reeve was not destined to outlive his patron Wordsworth by very long, and died on 10 May 1915 of a cerebral haemorrhage at his home, Yarrow Bank in Devon.[67] Following Reeve's death, the choir stalls he designed were dedicated, and a service was held to dedicate the nave. Reeve's partner and former clerk, W J Wilsdon, read the lesson, and Bishop Ridgeway 'paid warm tribute to the memory of Bishop Wordsworth with his far-sighted vision, and to Mr Reeve's skill and devotional spirit.'[68] Wilsdon, who wrote Reeve's RIBA obituary, described him as, 'A man of unassuming manner and high ideals, he never sought publicity, but he has left behind him some examples of his art which will be worthy memorials of a refined and artistic mind.'[69] Despite the fact that Reeve was a London architect, he always had a small practice, and consequently did not have the resources to enter many architectural competitions like his better-known contemporaries. Consequently his output of completed churches is small.

St Mark's Church, Salisbury. The crossing and east end.

Reeve made a speciality of carrying out church restorations, which, by their nature, generally only bring attention to the architects responsible if they are done very badly, and he does not appear to have been vilified in this respect! His textile designs are by their nature ephemeral, and the large amount of church fittings he designed have by the passing of time been disassociated with their creator. He seems to have enjoyed a good reputation as an architect during his lifetime, and in the early stages was no doubt helped by his associations with William Burges in forging links useful to a young architect starting a practice in London. Even more so, his sister's marriage into the Wordsworth family, brought him to the attention of Bishop Wordsworth, and his brother's friendship with Benson was a turning point for him.

No doubt many architects of the late 19th century, who were reasonably successful during their lifetime, suffer similar obscurity, but surely few can have boasted the connections that benefited Reeve, and the patronage he obtained as a consequence.

St Mark's Church, Salisbury. Exterior as built without the intended tower.

Notes

1 Wilsdon, W J, 'Obituary: The late Joseph Arthur Reeve', *RIBA Journal*, vol 22 (26 June 1915), p.426.
2 *Dictionary of British Architects 1834-1914* (London: Continuum, 2001), p.759.
3 Wornum, R Selden, 'Obituary Notice: Edward John Tarver, F.S.A., *RIBA Journal*, vol 7 (11 June 1891), p.360.
4 Brooks, C, *The Gothic Revival* (London: Phaidon, 1999), p.273.

5 Obituary of Joseph Arthur Reeve
6 Mordaunt-Crook, J, *William Burges and the High Victorian Dream* (London: Murray, 1981), p.80.
7 *ibid.*
8 Benson, A C, *The Life of Edward White Benson Sometime Archbishop of Canterbury* (London: Macmillan, 1899), p.523
9 *ibid*
10 *ibid.*
11 Obituary of Reverend Christopher Wordsworth, *Salisbury and Winchester Journal* (4 February 1938), p.11.

12 Marriage Certificate of Rev Christopher Wordsworth and Mary Reeve.

13 Reeve, J A, Bishop's Palace, Salisbury, Proposed Alterations (WSRO D1/31/8H)

14 Reeve, J A, 'Notes on the Architectural History of the Palace,' WANHM vol 25 (1890), pp.181-182.

15 RCHM, Salisbury: The Houses of the Close (London, 1993), p.72.

16 Reeve, op. cit. (1890), p.182.

17 Venables, Edmund, Episcopal Palaces of England (London: Isbister, 1895), p.172.

18 Wordsworth, J, 'The Bishop's Palace at Salisbury,' WANHM vol 25, p.167.

19 Reeve, op. cit. (1890), pp.181-189.

20 Thompson, Paul, William Butterfield (London: Routledge, 1971), p.443.

21 Now removed.

22 Baber, H, 'Restoration of Ramsbury Church', Salisbury Diocesan Gazette, vol 3 (1890), p.63.

23 Anon, 'Re-opening of Ramsbury Church', Salisbury Diocesan Gazette, vol 6 (1893), p.201.

24 Baber, loc. cit.

25 Cary, R N, Twelve Notable Good Women of the XIXth Century (London: Hutchinson, 1901), p. 161.

26 Anon, 'Re-opening of Ramsbury Church', Salisbury Diocesan Gazette, VI (1893), p.201. Anon, 'Re-opening of Ramsbury Church', Salisbury Diocesan Gazette, vol 6 (1893), p.201.

27 Faculty, Ramsbury church, 12 Dec 1890 (WSRO D1/61/35/1)

28 The last occasion when this had occurred was Bishop de la Wyle's founding of St Edmund's Church, Salisbury in 1268.

29 Shuttleworth, W, The People of God of St Marks (privately printed, 1992), p.5.

30 The proposed new Church in Salisbury: Minutes of meeting at the Council Chamber, p.3

31 Letter, Blomfield to Dugdale, 26 Sep 1890.

32 Letter, Micklethwaite to Wordsworth, 17 Nov 1890.

33 Letter, Harding to Dugdale, 22 Nov 1890.

34 McIlwain, John (ed.), All Saints Margaret Street (Andover: Pitkin, 1990), p.21.

35 Conditions of Competition for the post of Architect to the New District Church in the Parish of Milford, Salisbury.

36 Letter, Blomfield to Dugdale, 10 Nov 1890.

37 Letter, Blomfield to Dugdale, 26 Sept 1890.

38 Letter, Dugdale to Blomfield, 24 Sept 1890.

39 Letter, Blomfield to Dugdale, 26 Sept 1890.

40 Letter, Blomfield to Dugdale, 5 Feb 1891.

41 Report by Sir Arthur Blomfield on St Mark's Building Competition.

42 ibid.

43 Letter, Blomfield to Dugdale, 10 Feb 1891.

44 ibid.

45 ibid.

46 ibid.

47 Letter, Reeve to Dugdale, 16 Feb 1891.

48 Letter, Micklethwaite to Dugdale, 16 Feb 1891.

49 Letter, Bath to Dugdale, 20 Feb 1891.

50 Letter, Reeve to Dugdale, 16 Mar 1891.

51 Letter, Blomfield to Dugdale, 20 June 1891.

52 Anon, 'St Mark's Church, Salisbury: Dedication of the Nave', Salisbury Diocesan Gazette, vol 27 (1915), p.183.

53 Anon, 'St Mark's Church, Salisbury: Dedication of the New Church', Salisbury Diocesan Gazette, vol 7 (1894), p.119.

54 Letter, Reeve to Wyld, 6 Oct 1891.

55 Anon, 'S. Mark's Church, Salisbury: Laying of the Foundation stone by the Archbishop of Canterbury', Salisbury Diocesan Gazette, vol 5 (1892), p.104.

56 Letter, Reeve to Dugdale, 24 Aug 1891.

57 Letter, Reeve to Wyld, 19 Aug 1892.

58 Letter, Reeve to Wyld, 27 Apr 1893.

59 Wilsdon, W J, 'Obituary Notice: The late Joseph Arthur Reeve, RIBA

Journal, XXII (26 June 1915), p.426.

60 Reeve, J A, *The Builder,* (7 Nov 1885), p.183.

61 Wilsdon, *loc. cit.*

62 According to Reeve's R.I.B.A Journal obituary, he carried out painted decoration schemes in St Andrew's Westminster, St Stephen's Westminster, Luton Parish Church and St John's Hoxton. Pevsner noted in the latter that 'The surprise is the ambitious ceiling decoration of 1902-14 by J A Reeve, returned to its original vigour after cleaning in 1993-4: angels of the Apocalypse in square panels, on a blue background.' Cherry, B, and Pevsner, N, *Buildings of England, London 4: North* (London: Penguin, 1998), p.516.

63 Wilsdon, *loc. cit.*

64 Watson, E W, *Life of Bishop John Wordsworth* (London: Longman, 1915), p. 297.

65 Wilsdon,*loc. cit.*

66 Watson, *op. cit.*

67 Death Certificate of J A Reeve

68 Anon, 'S. Mark's, Salisbury: Dedication of the Nave', *Salisbury Diocesan Gazette,* vol 28 (1915), p.183.

69 Wilsdon, *loc. cit.*

Salisbury as a Seaport

Don Cross

In the *Hatcher Review* in 1995[1] John Chandler described the compelling story of John Taylor the Water Poet and his journey by wherry up the Salisbury Avon from Christchurch in 1623. But the use of the river for navigation begins much earlier, later passing through a commercial phase in the 17th and 18th centuries, and its use for boating is today still a matter of both fact and legal debate.

Early Times

It has long been suggested that the large Prescelly bluestones for Stonehenge were imported up-river from the sea – indeed the boys of Bryanston School demonstrated this possibility near Amesbury with a replica raft in 1953.[2] The Purbeck marble for Salisbury Cathedral also possibly came up-river from Christchurch in the 13th century. Weeds, shallows, mudbanks and fallen trees were no doubt major hindrances to river navigation on the Avon and other rivers but Christchurch Harbour was, according to O G S Crawford, 'the natural port for Wiltshire',[3] and Shortt, in his history of Salisbury, writes that the city built and manned a ship, *The Trout*, during the Hundred Years War, 'since the River Avon was navigable from Christchurch to Salisbury until the reign of Elizabeth I and so was technically a seaport'.[4] A right of passage was registered but there is little evidence that it was regularly enforced, and some other ships recorded as being linked to the city were probably boats owned and maintained by Salisbury merchants at Christchurch.[5]

The problems of inland transport became more acute in Tudor and Stuart times. River transport was becoming such an important economic alternative to the poor roads that, where possible, various schemes to improve navigation on most large rivers were proposed.[6] In 1535 the Commission for the River Avon was established[7] and Commissioners were appointed to remove weirs and obstructions, particularly where millers and landowners had forced boats to be dragged overland round barriers. Unfortunately, as in other areas, except on the largest rivers, nothing really changed.

The Navigation Debate Begins

The efforts of John Taylor vividly illustrate the opportunities for real commercial navigation of the river in the early 17th century – and there were others pressing the value of the Avon being made properly navigable around this time. Taylor pointed out that the Avon could be used to bring cheap wood fuel and charcoal from the New Forest for Salisbury's bellfoundries and even seacoal up-river from Christchurch, while beer, bricks, corn and wool could be carried down-river for export. One boat, he maintained, could carry 20 wagonloads of wood and could dispense with the need for 18 horses. Prophetically he commented: 'Methinks I see already men, horses, carts, mattocks, shovels, wheelbarrows, handbarrows and baskets at work clearing the river.'[8] Francis Mathew, in 1656, also had the same vision,[9] but the idea only began to become a reality with the Restoration of Charles II in 1660.

Possibly after a visit to Salisbury by the new king, city merchants and local nobility, including Lord Clarendon, Lord of the Manor of Twyneham (Christ-church), promoted an Act of Parliament in 1664 (16/17 Car. II P. A.) which became known as the Clarendon Act. This authorised work to begin making the Avon navigable from Christchurch to Salisbury and on to Wilton on the River Wylye if Lord Pembroke desired.[10] Much discourse took place in Salisbury but some of the landowners and millers along the river opposed the scheme. However, Christchurch built its Quay in 1671 and began to increase its coastal trade. In 1672 a pamphlet was published by John Hely promoting the develop-ment of the river navigation[11] and in 1675 another by 'R. S.' called 'Avona' in which Salisbury was optimistically envisaged as 'a second Bristol'.[12]

After much debate, and probably spurred on by Bishop Seth Ward, a founder member of the Royal Society, and recently translated to Salisbury from Exeter, Salisbury Corporation wrote to Lord Clarendon and offered a quarter of the cost to make the river navigable. In early 1675 Andrew Yarranton had surveyed the river at the request of the Earl of Salisbury. He agreed with Taylor's vision that the river could be made navigable and speculated that on completion, the cost of a load of timber could be reduced from £1 4s. 0d. to only four shillings by using river transport.[13]

The Navigators Set to Work

Enthusiasm began to grow and in July 1675 Salisbury City Corporation was further encouraged by its merchants and leading citizens to grant £2,000 and appoint a Committee of Management headed by Samuel Fortney. He received

£500 for another survey of the river, while Thomas Naish and John Mooring made a map or plan for £20 in August 1675.[14] It would seem probable that one of the leading proponents of the navigation scheme was Bishop Seth Ward[15] and it is just conceivable that it was his knowledge of the earliest use of pound locks on the Exeter Canal that led to their introduction on the Avon Navigation. It was he who, in the company of other local worthies, Mayor Smith, Lord Coleraine and Sir Thomas Mompesson, cut the first spit of the 'New Waterway' on 20 September 1675.[16]

Two or three hundred men began work digging the new channels and building locks (as at Britford which preserved Longford Castle weirs) and in November Salisbury's Mayor surveyed the progress. Sadly, lack of finance caused the City to withdraw its support in 1676 and several other sponsors and supporters defaulted or died.[17] There were problems and even fights over demolished weirs and new channels. In 1677 Salisbury Corporation suggested the Navigation construction undertakers be invited to carry on the work 'with any profits for ever' or until the Corporation redeemed the project at cost with 10% interest – an early form of Private/Public Partnership![18]

It would appear that the work continued nevertheless and in 1684 two 25-ton barges or wherries came up-river to Harnham Bridge. In 1685 three partners agreed to take over the project: Henry Hodges, a surgeon of the Cathedral Close, Thomas Dennett, a gentleman from Salisbury, and Thomas Bennet, a city grocer. The Navigation work was completed in 1687 when the Code of Navigation and Toll Charges were published.[19] The charge for carriage upstream from Christchurch to Salisbury was ten shillings a ton; downstream eight shillings per ton. Unloading costs, probably at both Christchurch Quay and at Salisbury Wharf were set at fourpence a ton.[20] Six years later, however, managers Robert Woodward, Wingfield Brockwell and Thomas Pitt were still at work on the Navigation, an Inspection was recorded in 1692 and a Report issued .[21]

In 1695 the Committee of Revenue was considering 'the discussion of matters touching the makeing of the river (Avon) navigable',[22] and in the same year, Celia Fiennes, during her late 17th century travels wrote that 'there has been a great attempt to make the Avon navigable, which would be of great advantage, but all charge has been lost in it'. She commented that a few barges had passed up-river but a flood had destroyed much of the works.[23]

Success and Failure

Information for this period is incomplete, but inevitably the weather at the turn of the century played a major part in these setbacks and we must assume that the severe flood damage of the years 1695–8, and particularly the Great Storm of 1703, made the Navigation unusable for several years, and that it was never fully restored due to lack of funds and the problems of the locks.

That it was navigable in the period 1680–95 and also probably between 1710–20 and boats sailed from Salisbury to Christchurch and vice versa is not in doubt. Documents from the Longford (Radnor) Estate[24] quote legal affidavits on Standlynch Mill waters, including the following:

> Robert Tanner . . . saith his father rented the mill at Standlynch for sixty years and the boatmen used to go through the weir-gap with their boats when the hatches were up, and when they were down, they used to haul their boats over the mead.
>
> Tho. Hatcher saith he was at the building of the Navigation bridges about thirty years ago (?1695) and he remembers barges about 45 years ago coming from Salisbury to Christchurch and from Christchurch to Salisbury for several years together; that . . . the navigation ceased and after some time was revived and the barges navigated as before. (?1710).
>
> Farmer Arnold. . . . remembers the barges navigating the river and coming through Standlinch where they were hauled through by windlass. . .

In 1698 a Parliamentary Bill was petitioned by Salisbury and others interested in the Navigation for an adjustment of the 1664 (Clarendon) Act. The Bill, claiming that defects in the original Act were hampering work on the Navigation, was opposed by the Mayor and Burgesses of Christchurch who said the undertakers 'did carry up some barges' but the riverside Petitioners claimed excessively heavy fines had been imposed for not cutting weeds. The Bill failed in Parliament.[25]

The End of the Dream

The decline of the Navigation continued as landowners began to construct complex and profitable water meadows along the valley. Mills reclaimed their weirs and sluices and the value of fishing rights rose. New bridges for improved roads began to cross the river, e. g. at Ringwood, and obstructed river transport. The large estate-owners and nobility in the Avon Valley saw little economic value in the Navigation and interest waned.

In 1724, however, further efforts were made to revive the Avon Navigation.[26] Canals were becoming the transport initiative and various decisions were made to form a new Committee. Daniel Defoe, in his travels in 1727, records that 'the Avon is still navigable to within two miles of Salisbury'.[27] In September 1729 Salisbury Corporation reconsidered the problem and decided to remit all arrears from the management of the Navigation if the Avon

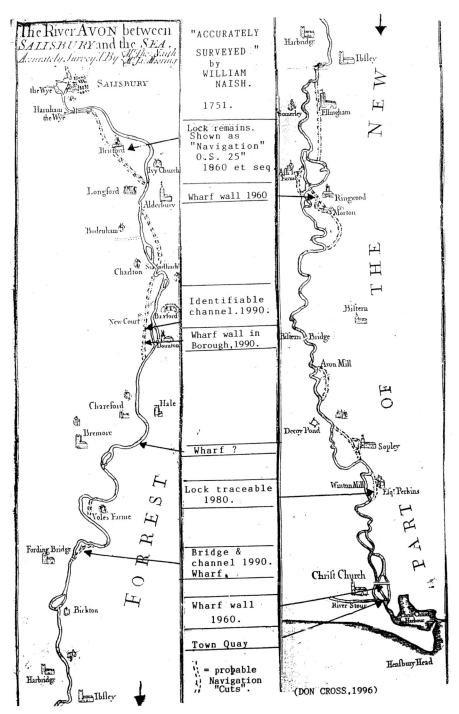

Fig 1: River Avon Navigation from Naish's map, 1751, with some remains still locatable in 1996 (author)

Fig 2: The only remaining pound lock on the Avon, at Britford (NGR SU 16278)

were again made navigable within five years. A further condition was that, if unsuccessful, the undertakers were to pay £20 a year until it was. Next year even these conditions were relaxed and Salisbury offered a thousand years ownership of the Navigation to whoever would go on with the task! Neither offer was accepted.[28]

William Naish produced a detailed map of Salisbury in 1716 with a revised edition in 1751.[29] This shows the line of the Avon Navigation between the city and the sea with the main channels and the navigation cuts (Fig 1). Francis Price in 1753 refers to barges and locks on the Avon, but says that the navigation scheme had been abandoned and Sir R Jervoise at Britford was using the locks there for irrigating his water meadows (Fig 2).[30] This lock remains recognisable and should be preserved by English Heritage as the only surviving example in 2003 of the Navigation made nearly 330 years ago.

Efforts were made in the 1770s to involve the entrepreneurs who were trying to complete the ill-fated Salisbury–Southampton Canal also to revive the Avon Navigation, but the failure of the Canal project meant that this last effort collapsed.[31]

The engineering problems of cutting and maintaining a sufficiently deep and controllable channel through the Avon Valley, especially south of Fordingbridge, were considerable. Drainage and flood controls did not exist at the time and the turnpike roads, and later railways, proved more economic.

Landowners, local fishing and other groups made sure that there was no revival of the boating interests. John Chandler's comment is unfortunately true: 'The Avon Navigation failed for two simple reasons – nobody wanted to look after it, and nobody wanted to use it'.[32]

Boats on the Navigation

The types of boats used when the Avon was commercially navigated are uncertain. We do know that boats were constructed along the River Avon below Sopley where barges were built in 'dry dock' in basins dug into the riverbank, rather after the fashion of John Constable's 19th-century painting of boat-building on the Essex Stour.[33] Words like 'barge' and 'wherry' appear in records but cover many types. Shallow draught sailing barges of some 10–30 tons capacity would seem the obvious choice since no footpaths or towpaths have been traced along the river. As some stretches were locked and 'canalised' with no strong currents, poling and sailing could be used, while along the main river

Fig 3: Wherry on the Avon at Salisbury, 18th-century oil painting by J Browne
(NSW Art Gallery, Sydney)

stretches movement would be more difficult, especially upstream in times of high river levels. It probably took at least two days to reach Salisbury from Christchurch but less down-river. Cargoes may have included salt, sea-coal, stone, timber, charcoal, iron goods, wheat and wines, up-river and wool, cloth, grain, cheese and beer downstream.

There are only rare illustrations of the Avon Navigation boats but overseas research by the author discovered an unknown painting in Australia in the Sydney New South Wales Art Gallery of at latest the 18th century which shows a wherry on the Avon near Salisbury (Fig 3).[34] Another painting, probably by the same artist, is in private hands in Sydney, and shows clearly a boat on the Navigation stretch at Britford – the same viewpoint which has been used in a recent redrawing by Michael Charlton in 1998 (Fig 4). An old print seen in Harbridge church in the 1960s is dated around 1800 and shows a small sailing boat on the Avon near Ibsley Bridge. Undoubtedly, there must be other old drawings and paintings surviving elsewhere.

Sailing on the Avon Today

Rowing boats can still be found on the Avon below Knapp Mill at Christchurch, at Ringwood, Fordingbridge and in Salisbury, but the riparian owners and fishing organisations and licensees refuse navigation on much of the Avon.

Fig 4: Wherry on the Avon Navigation near Britford, watercolour representation by Michael Charlton, 1998

Their permission has to be obtained for the occasional canoe race down-river or other water activities outside the urban areas. Legal challenges to assert the traditional right to use boats on the river above Christchurch in 1907–9 failed in the High Court for lack of support.[35] It was assumed that, despite the fact that the Clarendon Act has never been repealed, the legal right to navigate the river had lapsed by around 1900 or earlier with the waterway's collapse. The Act however does not specify whether the 'Navigation' was the river or the river plus the canalised channels as shown on Naish's 1751 map.[36] In any case the complete 'Navigation' line is not passable now since bridges have collapsed, water meadow sluices have replaced locks and many stretches have simply disappeared. Any legal challenge today to reassert the right of navigation along our Salisbury Avon to and from the sea would certainly be both long and costly!

References and Endnotes

1   Chandler, John (1995) 'John Taylor makes a voyage to Salisbury', *Hatcher Review*, vol 4 no 40, 19-34.

2   *Salisbury Journal*, 10 Jul 1953.

3   Crawford, O G S (1953), *Archaeology in the Field*, 78-86. Crawford, O G S (1912), 'Distribution of Early Bronze Age Settlement', *Geographical Jnl*, Aug/ Sept, 196.

4   Shortt, Hugh (ed) (1957) *City of Salisbury*, 49.

5   Letter from F D Lane of Christchurch 5 Feb 1958 quoting lecture by H Pye-Smith to Salisbury Chartered Surveyors' group (1926).

6   Willan, T S (1936) *River Navigation in England*, Oxford; Taylor, E (1930) *Late Tudor and Early Stuart Geography*, Methuen, 119-120.

7   *Henry VIII/20* (1535) British Museum Library.

8   Chandler, *op. cit.* Also quoted by Willan, T S (1937) 'Salisbury and the navigation of the Avon', *WANHM*, vol 47, 592-4.

9   Mathew, F (1656) *On the Openeing of Rivers* R H L 2. (Quoted by Aubrey, J (1847) *The Natural History of Wiltshire* (ed. John Britton), 3).

10 Act published in *Christchurch Miscellany*, July 1922, 165.

11 Hely, J(1672) *A modest representation*, London.

12 'R S' (1675) *Avona*, Salisbury (pamphlet). See also Willan, T S *op cit.* and Aubrey, J *op cit.* 28 and Gough's *Topography* vol 2, 366.

13 Yarranton, A (1675) *England Improv'd*, 1, 42, 67. Aubrey (*op. cit.*) suggests that the commencement of works was on 20 September 1675 and Britton [Aubrey's editor] adds the date 1669 and later an incomplete 16. . . for full commitment. Should this incomplete date be 1675? Britton's insertion suggests that the initial commencement with the Salisbury Mayor's Committee of Management 'to consult and treat with such persons as will undertake to tender the Avon navigable' was in 1669. (Aubrey, *op cit*, 28).

14 Historic Manuscripts Commission. *Report on MSS in various collections*, vol 4, 247. See also Hatcher H (1843) *Old and New Sarum*, 460, 497.

15 Chandler, John (*1983) Endless Street*, Hobnob Press, 136.

16 Report, (Oct 4/7 1675) *London Gazette*.

17 H M C *op. cit*, 247. See also Hatcher *op. cit.* 460, 497.

18 *Calendar SPD* 1693, 33.

19 *Calendar of Treasury Bks* vol 8, pt 3, 250 refs (Also ref. in Aubrey, *op cit.* 28)

20 The location of Salisbury Wharf is the subject of some debate. John Taylor in 1623 disembarked from his wherry just beyond Fisherton Bridge near the site of the present King's Head Inn.

21 Calendar *SPD* 1693, 34.

22 H M C *op.cit*, 251.

23 Fiennes, C *The illustrated journeys of Celia Fiennes c. 1682-c.*1712, 46; and *VCH Hampshire*, vol 5, 452.

24 WSRO 490/1683.

25 There has been much debate and scepticism about whether barges did navigate up and down the Avon at this time, but the legal evidence quoted here (note 24) supports the other evidence that it was indeed used. Other supporting references include: Hadfield, C *Canals of Southern England*, 354-355; Bell, Nancy, *Harbour to Harbour*, Christchurch, 1935, 46; and Willan, T (*op. cit.*). Booth-Jones, N, *History of Hale and Woodgreen* (1953), 19, states that two 25-ton barges went up to Salisbury in 1684. Hatcher (*op. cit.*) writes that this was 'before 25th December 1685'. Willan quotes Defoe (*op. cit.*) that it was made navigable and includes the Avon in 1687 in his list of navigable rivers (1660–1700) quoting *Cal Treasury Books* vol 8, pt 3, 120, and the *Journal of the House of Commons* The Royal Commission on Canals and Waterways *Report* 1906-09, vol 1, 358 Q 10, 877 says that the Navigation was used for a short time. How many of these are requoting previous sources is unknown. Hannen, R, *History of Fordingbridge*, 52 quotes Dr Pope's *Salisbury Ballad* about Bishop Ward who brought vessels to Salisbury. Priestley, J (1831), *Historical account of navigable canals and rivers*, 452, states clearly that 'this river was made navigable from Christchurch to Salisbury'.

26 Willan, T S *op. cit.*

27 Defoe, D (1724-1727), *Tour through the whole island of Great Britain*.

28 Willan, T S, (1937).

29 Naish,W *Map of Salisbury*, (1751 ed)

30 Hannen, R, *History of Fordingbridge*, 24.

31 Chandler, John, *op.cit.*, 130.

32 *ibid*.

33 Bell, Nancy, *op. cit.*, l42-7.

34 The New South Wales Art Gallery has this painting's provenance as: *J Browne, Landscape with view of Salisbury Cathedral, oil on canvas 63. 2x78 cms., l8th century. Gift of Mrs Anna Hills sister of late John Henry Challis, 1899.* (Photo. copyright). Its viewpoint is uncertain but would appear to be above Downton Road. The other painting is in the ownership of another resident of Sydney.

35 *Christchurch Times,* 19 Oct 1907, 29 Feb 1908 and 15 May 1909 (Red House Museum, Christchurch library). Oakley, R, (1920) *Guide to Christchurch*, 63. Many local newspapers carry records of various 'water carnivals' and regattas during the summers in the 18th, 19th, and 20th centuries at Salisbury, Downton, Fordingbridge and Ringwood (e.g. *Salisbury Journal, Fordingbridge suppt*, 27 Mar, 2003).

36 For the industrial archaeology survey of the remains of the Navigation, see Cross, D A E (2001) *Salisbury as a Seaport*, Wessexplore, Salisbury. For general economics see Cross, D A E, (1960), unpublished MA thesis on *Economic Geography of Hampshire Avon Basin*, University of London Library.

'Saved to Serve':
Fallen Women in Salisbury

John Elliott

S adly few pay much attention to the little range of recently restored buildings connected to Salisbury College which are on the eastern side of Churchill Way, yet historically they are some of the most significant in Salisbury. Before St Osmund's church was built in 1848, the northernmost block was home to Salisbury's small Roman Catholic community, and it was here that the Gothic Revivalist A. W. N. Pugin converted to Catholicism. When the Catholics moved out an Anglican Penitentiary moved in and the buildings provided the focus for nineteenth century campaigns to save fallen women.

In Victorian Britain women were either elevated as moral exemplars or condemned because they failed to live up to these standards. For a man, women were either sent to save or to ruin, and while most men claimed that they preferred their women to be of the idealised saving type they were, none the less, fascinated by the fallen and the ruined.[1] A double standard existed which John Ruskin justified in his *Sesame and Lilies*:

> The man, in his rough work in open world, must encounter all peril and trial; – to him, therefore, must be failure, the offence, the inevitable error . . . But he guards the woman from all this; within his house, as ruled by her, unless she herself has sought it, need enter no danger, no temptation, no cause of error or offence.[2]

So a married man who deviated from the moral high ground was to be pitied and forgiven as it was no more than was to be expected because of the risks he undertook. A wife who deviated was deemed to have invited the evil, was made a social outcast, expelled from the home and often forced into prostitution as a means of supporting herself.

Yet, such females were also attractive as they enabled men to combine the respectability of married life with the pleasures of illicit sex, while also providing a male solution to the middle class practice of late marriages – a kept woman bridging the gap between youth and respectability.

However, if Thomas Hardy and his *Ruined Maid* is to be believed, ruination was not all bad.

'O'Melia, my dear, this does everything crown!
Who could have supposed I should meet you in Town?
And whence such fair garments, such prosperi–ty?' –
'O didn't you know I'd been ruined?' said she.

– You left us in tatters, without shoes or socks,
Tired of digging potatoes, and spudding up docks;
And now you've gay bracelets and bright feathers three!' –
'Yes. That's how we dress when we're ruined', said she.

Prostitution also supplemented poorly paid employment. It provided a way past an economic system that limited women's opportunities for work and constrained them to the subsistence end of the market. William Acton, author of *Prostitution, Considered in Its Moral, Social and Sanitary Aspects* (1857), believed that poverty was the chief cause of prostitution and Henry Mayhew, in his *London Labour and the London Poor* (1851-2), agreed.

A desire to change things and to reform the fallen has its roots in the eighteenth century and the opening of the Magdalen Hospital in London in 1758. Over the next sixty years other establishments followed in various provincial cities,[3] and by the late 1840s there were eight such places in London and 13 elsewhere in England.

It is difficult to ascertain the scale of prostitution. Police statistics of 1860 show about 30,000 known prostitutes in England, while, in 1882, the Church Penitentiary Association claimed that there were at least 50,000 in London alone. However, whatever the statistics the scale was seen as sufficiently large

Clewer exterior
The chapel was designed by Henry Woodyer and built between 1878-81. Woodyer was responsible for two buildings in Salisbury, St Edmund's schools in Bedwin Street (1859-60) and Fisherton Anger School (1867-8). He also restored and extended St John the Baptist at Berwick St John (1861-2), enlarged St Swithin at Compton Bassett by adding a new chancel (1865-6) as well as designing the memorial fountain in the Market Place at Devizes (1879).

Clewer interior
This was the focus of convent life though it is now awaiting a new life as a developer converts the other convent buildings into flats. As a grade 2* building it has to be preserved. Woodyer designed a similarly grand chapel at All Saints Hospital, Eastbourne (1873-4).

to require some special response by the Church of England.[4]

In 1848 the Rev John Armstrong wrote the first of several articles which proposed the creation of religious penitentiaries run by sisterhoods, in contrast to the existing establishments that were run by well-meaning married women.[5] In 1852 the Church Penitentiary Association was formed as a result of Armstrong's activities. This organisation went on to provide the focus for a growing number of church establishments whose primary focus was the salvation of fallen women.[6] However, it should be noted that these places were for the salvation of childless women, the Union Workhouse being seen as a more suitable place for the less fortunate who also had the care of a child.

Three establishments are usually cited as the earliest church penitentiaries – the House of Mercy at Clewer near Windsor (1849), the House of Peace in North Road Plymouth (1850) and the House of Mercy at Bussage (1851). Rarely is Salisbury recognised as being in the vanguard of both secular and religious attempts to address this problem, yet it was a leader whose contribution to this reform work deserves to be better recognised.

As early as 1831 the Wilts Female Penitentiary Association had been formed and acquired De Vaux Lodge, just outside the Harnham Gate to Salisbury Cathedral. Here, according to the *Salisbury & Winchester Journal*, there would be 'an asylum to that unhappy class of our fellow creatures whose melancholy situation necessarily renders them outcasts of society'.[7] The founders included Bishop Thomas Burgess and the Dowager Countess of Pembroke. The intention was that up to twelve girls would be accommodated and receive help from certain of the respectable philanthropic ladies of The Close. Why the Salisbury home was so early in the process is unclear. Perhaps it was a result of an Army presence, perhaps the consequence of some active reformers living in Salisbury.

Whatever the reason the Salisbury institution predates most of the better known establishments.

The first two girls were admitted on 27 October 1831. Anne Mould was aged 17 and Mary Ann Beale was just 15. Both stayed until February 1834 before going into service. It was not just the young who were admitted. Charlotte Hill, a 46 year old married woman, entered the home on 17 December 1831 and remained there till 25 October 1832 when she returned to her husband, a seaman, who had paid 2/– a week for her keep.[8]

During the first 10 years of its operation the Salisbury home attracted a steady flow of girls, viz:[9]

Year	No admitted		
1831	3	1835	5
1832	6	1836	7
1833	6	1837	8
1834	6	1838	4
		1839	7

Between 1839-50 some 89 women were admitted, 52 under the age of 20, some of whom had 'scarcely attained the tender age of fourteen', and a further 20 who were under 23 years of age. Most seem to have stayed for about two years and then went into service or to friends, though some left of their own accord, and a few were expelled because of bad conduct. Elizabeth Greene

Buildings in Churchill Way
Before the erection of St Osmund's church in Exeter Street in 1848 this was home to Salisbury's Roman Catholics and where A. W. N. Pugin converted to Roman Catholicism. Then it was taken over by the Anglican Wilts Female Penitentiary Association and provided Salisbury's focus for the attempt to save fallen women as well as a central laundry facility. It is now part of Salisbury College.

from Milford, entered the home aged 18 on 17 June 1850 and was thrown out, or in the more polite words of the Refuge Register, 'Left for bad conduct', on 2 December 1850.[10]

Clearly the promoters believed that the operation had been a success, as in 1850 they claimed that women who were engaged in a 'life of sin and wretchedness' were 'now filling responsible stations in society, as wives, mothers, or domestic servants.'[11]

The accounts for 1849/50 show that it cost £305 to run the home, only £30 of which went as salaries, and that the operation was financed by subscriptions and donations (£192) and a commercial laundry operation (£94).[12]

Salisbury's Roman Catholics had worshipped from a building in St Martin's Church Street until 1848 when they moved to St Osmund's Church in Exeter Street. The Wilts Female Penitentiary Association acquired the old building and moved the refuge there from De Vaux Place, renaming it St Martin's Home. Perhaps a location less adjacent to the Cathedral held attractions and in any event the new site offered better accommodation and a modest increase in the numbers followed:[13]

Year	No admitted
1852	8
1853	13
1854	10
1855	8
1856	7

The 1854 report claimed that there was an average of 13 girls in the home throughout the year. Of the nine that had left in that year, five had gone into service and four had returned to their families 'in consequence of not conforming to the rules of the house'. The same report also highlighted the growing impor-tance of the laundry operation: subscriptions and donations at £207 were little changed from five years earlier but the revenue from laundry work had increased from £94 to £165 11s. 5d., with needlework adding another £14 10s. 10d.[14]

While the Church Penitentiary Association favoured the kind of operation which was established at Bussage (1851) and Clewer (1849), whereby the whole operation would be part of a religious community run by nuns, in its earlier years the Salisbury operation appears to have been staffed by married ladies.

Towards the end of the 1860s it appears that the sponsors of the Salisbury Penitentiary decided to switch from an institution run by lay ladies to one operated by sisters. In 1871 the home became the Salisbury Diocesan House of Mercy for Reclaiming the Fallen – a title charged with meaning – and between 1870-8 the

Bussage sisters took control of day-to-day operations. However, there is also evidence of financial difficulties about this time. An appeal dated 10 June 1871 claimed that the cost of maintaining twelve girls and the necessary staff was £370 a year, of which £135 could be recovered from laundry work, leaving £235 of which only £180 was covered by donations.[15] In 1878 there was a return to lay control when Mrs Macnamara and others ran the operation for about four years. The 1881 census records Katherine Macnamara (aged 41) and Esther Cooper (aged 37) plus two teenage relations, two visitors and three servants along with five 'penitent' girls whose average age was just over 20 and who had originated from places as diverse as Newcastle, Greatham, Norwich and Salisbury.[16]

Then in 1889 the home came under the umbrella of the Clewer sisters, and it was as an outpost of the Windsor convent that the Salisbury operation moved forward into the twentieth century, being significantly enlarged along the way.[17] This change of control is not as surprising as it may appear. The Clewer Convent had become a national centre for such work and its sisters were seen as the experts. Quickly the Clewer operation fostered a series of local refuges that filtered the girls between those seeking temporary respite and those who wanted genuinely to find a new life.

An agreement was reached with the Clewer sisters on 1 October 1888 whereby the Salisbury committee would provide funds to pay for two sisters, two matrons and twelve girls. The operation would be renamed St Mary's Home, and Mother Jane Francis confirmed the agreement in a letter to the Bishop dated 17 November 1888. The two Clewer sisters arrived on 15 January 1889.

Almost instantly the scale of the operation was increased. A new laundry was added along with two large dormitories and eight rooms for the sisters and supervisory staff. The potential number of girls who could be accommodated rose from 14 to 40 and the enlarged home opened for business on 2 February 1890.[18] The basement was given over to the laundry. On the ground floor there were kitchens, a dining room and a large dormitory that would hold sixteen along with separate bedrooms for the sisters and other staff. The first floor had a large sewing room, another dining room with refectory tables and another dormitory plus private bedrooms. There was a small second floor section at the northern end and this contained yet another dormitory.[19]

In 1889, immediately before the Clewer sisters took over, the laundry operation raised £218 5s. 5d. a year. The new expanded laundry followed and by 1909/10 the annual value of this operation had increased to £1,079 17s. 5d.[20] Clearly washing away the grime of life was as beneficial as washing away the sins of immorality!

After the Clewer sisters took control the numbers did increase but not by as much as might have been expected, viz:[21]

Year	No admitted
1889	11
1890	10
1891	4
1892	19

From now on the Salisbury establishment would act as a feeder home for Clewer. Typical was Elisabeth Stephens, who, aged 16, was admitted to the Salisbury home on 22 September 1890. Like many others she had a father and step-mother, and 'Got amongst bad companions'. She stayed at Salisbury until 12 October 1892 before moving to Clewer where she continued her rehabilitation and was 'doing well in service Feb/97.'

The (undated) Salisbury rules forbade the girls from ever speaking to one another about 'past wrong doing'. They were allowed to write to their relations at least once a month, plus 'extra letters with leave from the Clewer Sister. An extra letter can always be earned by good behaviour'. However, 'All letters are read and sealed by the Sister Superior and letters that come to them are opened by the Sister Superior'. Visits seem to have been discouraged, as 'Relations may be allowed to see them once in three months with permission from the Sister Superior and if necessary in the presence of one of the Sisters.'[22]

Any respectable penitentiary required a chapel that would be the spiritual focus of the home, and at Clewer the sisters had commissioned Henry Woodyer to design a magnificent chapel. In Salisbury they asked G. H. Gordon, a local man, to do somewhat the same, though on a much smaller scale.

The chapel was erected on the northern end of the complex. Built of red brick and Doulting stone in the Early English style, there was room for 90 with stalls for 14 sisters.[23] Bishop John Wordsworth laid the foundation stone on 8 July 1893 as a memorial to Christopher Pleydell-Bouverie, a past secretary and treasurer and a son of the Earl of Radnor. There seems to have been much celebrating and a large audience, including most of the local clergy and aristocracy. The Bishop dedicated the completed chapel on Monday 2 April 1894. The Clewer sisters produced the altar frontal and the three eastern windows were glazed with stained glass depicting Our Lady, St John the Baptist and Isaiah.[24]

About the same time the liturgy also took on a more 'advanced' format. The Oxford Movement had advocated a more 'catholic' ethos but there was always a fear that excess could lead to the return to what were considered 'Popish' practices. Yet within striking distance of the Cathedral, the Chaplain, the Rev H. W. Carpenter, openly described how, 'I use lights, mixed chalice, and coloured stoles, &c.' while a statue of the Virgin stood in the chapel; all practices which were a step too far for many Anglicans.

St Mary's continued to be run by the Clewer sisters until 1947, and the numbers admitted continued to increase.[25]

Altar front
Designed by Bodley & Hare in 1930 this altar front depicts three scenes from Mary's
life: the annunciation, nativity and assumption to heaven.

Year	No admitted		
1915	27	1932	23
1916	18	1933	18
1917	13		
1918	19	1945	26
		1946	24
1931	16	1947	15

There were more building plans around 1930,[26] as the complex was again enlarged but the client group seems to have changed little. Typical was Florence May Clapman who entered the home on 5 October 1915 because she had 'been fallen' for 18 months. She had a mother and step-father and her mother had a drink problem.[27]

Throughout the nineteenth century most girls were sent to the home by moral welfare workers in Wiltshire, Dorset and Hampshire. The girls were usually aged between 16 and 25 and typically stayed in the home for one or two years, during which time they received 'character training' from a dedicated sister-teacher. Throughout, the emphasis was on saving the girl from her immoral ways so that she could go on to serve others in service: she was being 'saved to serve'.

However, it seems that the concept of the fallen woman started to be eroded shortly after World War II. From 1947 St Mary's became a home for the 'training of girls from school-leaving age to twenty-one', 'girls of normal mentality who are difficult or mal-adjusted, or who come from bad homes or unsatisfactory surroundings.' It was also recognised by the Home Office as 'a residence for girls on probation.' Perhaps the girls were little different from their predecessors, just that the label 'fallen woman' had been replaced with the labels 'difficult or maladjusted'. Whatever the label, the medicine that was offered remained largely unchanged, and concentrated on 'training in housework, cooking and sewing'.

The emergence of a State funded Welfare Service meant that St Mary's eventually became redundant and, in 1952, unsuccessful efforts were made to find a new religious use for the buildings. For a short while they were used by St Andrew's Home from Portsmouth as a temporary replacement for their bomb damaged premises. The Samaritans followed, as did the Salisbury & Wells Theological College, but in 1978 the buildings passed to Salisbury College and started a long period of structural decline. However, during 2002/3 builders started converting the penitentiary complex into student accommodation and the chapel into a staff room through a mix of new-build and restoration.

Surely this is historically one of Salisbury's most important buildings. It was here that Pugin converted to Roman Catholicism and set about his attempts to turn England back to a pre-Reformation past. The penitentiary which was created in De Vaux Lodge was one of the earliest such establishments in the United Kingdom and its successor in St Martin's Church Street played an important part in the nineteenth century campaign to save the fallen. As such, a Blue Plaque seems to be the least that is required to mark the site of such notable activities.

Select bibliography:

Susan Mumm, *Stolen Daughters, Virgin Mothers Anglican Sisterhoods in Victorian Britain* (1999)

Susan Mumm, '"Not Worse than Other Girls": The Convent-Based Rehabilitation of Fallen Women in Victorian Britain' in *Journal of Social History* vol 29 (1996).

Penitentiary Work in the Church of England (1873).

'The Ruined Maids of Windsor' in John Elliott and John Pritchard, *Henry Woodyer Gentleman Architect* (2002, pp. 93-108.

Notes

1 The fallen comprised those woman who were sexually active outside marriage, whether willingly or under duress.

2 John Ruskin, *Sesame and Lilies* (1894), pp. 107-8.

3 Including Exeter, Bristol, Norwich, Liverpool and Leeds.

4 By the end of the nineteenth century there were 238 penitentiaries and feeder refuges associated with the Church Penitentiary Association, over 200 of which were run by sisterhoods, with room for 7,000 women. The Reformatory & Refuge Union had 320 institutions by 1908. I am grateful to John Pritchard for this information and for much of the general information on the development of this movement.

5 For an account of the formation of Anglican religious communities in the nineteenth century see A. M. Allchin, *The Silent Rebellion: Anglican Religious Communities 1845-1900* (1958) and Peter. F. Anson, *The Call of the Cloister* (1964).

6 While the Church Penitentiary Association favoured sisterhoods, the Reformatory & Refuge Union, which was formed in 1856 as a non-denominational body, was more supportive of secular control.

7 *Salisbury & Winchester Journal* 26 December 1831.

8 WSRO D401/3.

9 Ibid.

10 Ibid.

11 WSRO D401/1.

12 A further £13 14s.4d. came from a commercial needlework business. See WSRO D401/1.

13 WSRO D401/3.

14 WSRO D401/1.

15 WSRO D401/1.

16 I am grateful to Jane Howells for pointing this out to me.

17 The community at Clewer was particularly important, not just because of its size, but also because it acted as a focus for a range of subsidiary refuges, many of which were in London. Typical of its type, it was started by a crusading clergyman, the Rev Thomas Carter and two reforming ladies, Mariquita Tennant who opened a refuge in her Windsor home and Harriet Monsell, a 40 year old widow, who became a nun and the first leader of the Clewer Sisterhood. Between 1853 and 1893 some combination of Carter, Monsell and the architect Henry Woodyer created a purpose built convent complex on the outskirts of Windsor. The convent finally closed in 2002, the sisters having spent much of their latter days caring for the elderly.

18 WSRO D401/9.

19 See plans of existing and proposed building which were produced by Bodley & Hare in 1930.

20 £962 in 1907/8, £876 in 1905/6. The laundry was enlarged again in 1923.

21 WSRO D401/3.

22 WSRO D401/9.

23 It cost £1,200.

24 The glazing in these windows was later replaced by Kempe glass in 1929. Kempe glass was also added to other windows between 1895 and 1903.

25 WSRO D401/4.

26 A drawings by Bodley & Hare dated 26.5.1930 is held in the WSRO D401/9. A dormitory block was added in 1927.

27 She went on to be sent to Bermondsey.

A Theatre Fit for the New Millennium

Hugh Abel and Sue Johnson

Studio Theatre can trace its origins to the drama section of the Salisbury War Workers' Recreational Centre. This organisation, formed in the early 1940s to cater for the leisure needs of those drafted into war work in the district, produced plays in the Centre's premises in Blue Boar Row and various Salisbury halls. In 1946 with the winding up of the Centre its drama section became 'The Centre Players Amateur Dramatic Society'. Plays such as *The Rivals* and *Arms and the Man* were performed at the Arts Theatre in Fisherton Street, in hospitals and in local villages.

By 1950 it became apparent that the time was ripe for a bold experiment in amateur drama based on the idea of a small intimate 'studio' theatre run on club lines. In the winter of that year three one-act plays were produced at the *London Hotel* in front of a small invited audience. Encouraged by the success of this venture Priestley's *They Came to a City* ran for a week the following year. With a membership of more than 200 the search then started for a permanent home. In the autumn of 1951 premises were found in Milford Street when a disused wine store at the *Milford Arms Inn* [now *The Old Coach House*] was leased on an annual basis from Gibbs Mew Brewery. Led by Oliver and Mary Godfrey, and with the help and encouragement of Mr Peter Gibbs, the Centre Players set about transforming the premises into a theatre.

Members put in many hours of hard work but it then became obvious that major structural repairs were necessary. This led to inevitable delays and during a wet winter rain ruined much of the volunteers' work, including the scenery. However, by autumn 1952 work was complete giving an auditorium with seating for 65 and a stage with the facility to 'fly' scenery – the first of its kind in Salisbury. The theatre was reached via a small foyer and staircase, with changing rooms, workshop and scenery store on the floor above. The first production there at the end of October was *Amphitryon 38*, a comedy by Jean Giraudoux, which received a favourable review in the *Salisbury Journal*.

The following year the prefix 'Centre Players' was dropped and Studio Theatre Club was born, to begin its long reputation as a company producing high calibre drama. In 1954 Nobel Prize winner William Golding directed the *Alcestis* of Euripides while the summer of 1958 saw an exciting new venture – open air theatre. In a joint venture with The Avon Valley Players, Shakespeare's *Twelfth Night* was produced on the lawns of Church House, Crane Street, Salisbury, to raise funds for the Eventide Centre and Studio Theatre's chair appeal.

In 1958 Studio's achievements were recognised when it was invited to become a member of the Little Theatre Guild of Great Britain, a prestigious organisation of independently owned small theatres who enjoy national recognition in the arts world.

When the *Milford Arms* was sold by Gibbs Mew in 1964 Studio had to quit the premises. Meetings and rehearsals continued in The Loft, in the grounds of the *Swan Inn* [now the *Greyfisher*] in Ayleswade Road, with performances at the College of Technology. When the College theatre became unavailable another venue at St Thomas church was found, and later plays were presented at the [new] Playhouse.

The late 1970s provided a challenging period when Salisbury Arts Centre was established and the new Playhouse opened with a studio space of its own. Both venues launched vigorous appeals for financial support and both began to attract touring companies producing the kind of drama previously provided locally by Studio Theatre. In spite of this competition Studio remained a popular venue for audiences from all parts of Wiltshire and Hampshire. Efforts to find suitable premises continued, including negotiations with Salisbury Museum for the use of its lecture theatre.

In 1978 when the premises at the *Swan Inn* were due for redevelopment Studio moved into the stable block at the rear of the *Railway Tavern* in South Western Road. Compared with previous locations The Stables were ideal in many ways, but could seat just 40 people and performances were still only for club members and their guests. By 1980 Studio was no nearer its goal of a site on which to build its own 'little theatre' (already designed by Anthony Stocken, a local architect) but the dream came one step closer when in 1984 the former Air Training Corps huts in Ashley Road were purchased. Following a great deal of hard work these were transformed into an intimate 50-seater theatre which opened for business in January 1985 with a performance of *Mixed Doubles*. For almost 20 years these converted wartime military huts were to provide Studio Theatre with a permanent home.

For more than 40 years Studio Theatre has provided quality drama and encouraged and supported not only its membership but also local community groups to participate in projects both on a local and a national scale. Members

The old theatre

come from all ages and all occupations – from the medical, teaching and judicial professions to students and families. Many have gone on to work in professional theatre or television. As an amateur-run organisation Studio Theatre functions as an affordable leisure amenity for the community, and while striving for high standards of production, is not restricted by commercial considerations. This enables it to include in its programme revivals of popular large cast classics which are now beyond the means of most professional theatres due to high costs.

It mounts five or six full-scale productions a year including premieres of work by award winning writers of national stature such as John Godber and Debbie Issitt. There are also themed evenings, revue-style entertainments and rehearsed readings devised as fund-raisers. The annual open-air production, often Shakespeare, at venues like Old Sarum, the Cathedral School, or Downton Moot is something of an adventure with the uncertain weather and hazards in the form of low flying aircraft.

In addition Studio takes an active role in arts and community events in Salisbury, eg fundraising for the new Playhouse (1974) and the Spire Appeal (1986). In the last five years activities have included participating in the St George's Day celebrations, entertaining at Guildhall open days, running children's workshops in schools, hiring out costumes for plays, pantomimes and fancy dress, taking part in local radio productions, and becoming part of the Salisbury Arts Strategy Group. The current President is Rosemary Squires. Past Presidents include Sir Reginald Kennedy Cox, Noreen Salberg and David Horlock.

Although the Ashley Road huts provided a permanent home they were obviously not ideal. The constant need for external weather-proofing of ageing wooden buildings was a heavy financial burden, not to mention problems with security. Eventually time took its toll, insurance could not be obtained, and without complete rewiring a Licence for Public Performance would not be given. Fundraising had started in 1993, and the 1995-6 programme had re-iterated Studio's desire to a purpose built theatre on the site. In 1997 the decision had been made to replace the old huts with a new building with a seating capacity of 100. However the project faced many obstacles. Although Studio owned the wooden huts the site is leased from Salisbury District Council and the process of getting the necessary permissions and applying for grants was lengthy and complicated. A 25-year lease was finally granted but further delays were caused because the location is part of an old landfill site. The local authority therefore required an evaluation study to establish if contaminants were present and whether or not any harmful substances might leach down into the aquifer. This process took several months and whilst trace elements were detected, little remedial action was required.

The estimated cost of the new theatre is £250,000. Substantial financial commitment has come from Salisbury District Council, the Foundation for Sports and the Arts, Southern Arts lottery fund, Waitrose, and some grant aiding trusts together with Studio's own fund raising efforts. By the spring of 2001 sufficient funding was in place for work to begin. During January 2002 the building was cleared and costumes etc moved to temporary storage; then the

The new theatre takes shape, March 2003 (photo: Sue Johnson)

following month the bulldozers moved in to clear the site. Construction started in January 2003 and by mid March the steel framework was in place.

Designed by John Coleman, a local architect, the new building will be multi-functional. It is intended to provide Salisbury with a permanent amateur theatre, supporting the work of a thriving amateur dramatic group and serving the cultural needs of a wider community, including those with physical and learning disabilities and mental health problems. Thus as well as a venue for Studio's own productions, it will offer performance space to small-scale professional companies and youth drama groups, rehearsal space to professional companies such as Salisbury Playhouse and meeting/conference facilities for local groups and businesses. It should also provide a much-needed additional location for events during Salisbury Festival. The target date for re-opening is January 2004, funding permitting!

References

Salisbury Journal
1952, Oct 10, p9 and Oct 31, p8.
1985, Jan 17, p14.
1993, Feb 21, p7.
Salisbury Times
1958, Jly 18, p14.

Salisbury Local Studies Library ephemera collection, especially 79.2/STU and SAL 792.

New Theatre Appeal Brochure (undated).

William Small's Memoir

Steve Hobbs

Personal accounts of the lives of working people are extremely rare in any century and one of a painter and glazier in 19th-century Salisbury in two volumes running to 736 closely written pages is likely to cause much interest in Wiltshire. The memoir appeared in an auctioneer's catalogue in spring 2003 and has been acquired by the Wiltshire & Swindon Record Office (catalogue number WSRO 2713/2). In 1881 William Small sat down and wrote about his life, his family and acquaintances and his home city. These subjects were embellished with poetry and items of interest from the national press, together with historical notes on Salisbury from published works. Although these account for quite a large part of the books nevertheless there is much of considerable interest to local and family historians. As well as writing about people he knew, such as tradesmen, apprentices and inhabitants of the Close he gives much useful information about houses, many of which he worked on. Harnham House we are told was built in 1831 and its owner and tenants for the next 15 years are named.

Small's historical interests led him to include many items of news from the years 1737–8 which must come from the *Salisbury and Winchester Journal*. Since no complete file for this year is available in the United Kingdom it is possible that some of the snippets have come from papers not ready accessible to researchers today.

Reading through the Memoir it is impossible not to appreciate the melancholic nature of the author. By 1881 he appears to have outlived all his family and he expresses his sense of loneliness and emptiness over many pages. To modern taste he appears over-sentimental and maudlin but the Victorians' preoccupation with death, all too present in their lives, is well documented and we should not be surprised in the tone of the writing. This adds another dimension to the Memoir in what it reveals about the writer's thoughts and beliefs.

Bishopdown:
the Missing Links
Peter Hart

Bishopdown was formerly part of the bishop's manor of Milford and Woodford, which totalled 857 hectares.[1] 'In 1860 the leasehold interest was bought by the Ecclesiastical Commissioners for over £43,000'.[2]

In 1911 the City Council sent a deputation to the Commissioners to ask whether they would consider leasing land for a golf links, to be run by the Municipality when the Bishopdown estate was developed: 'It would help to sell sites for residences of a superior class'.[3] Cluttons, the agents for the Commissioners, reacted favourably to the idea;[4] so the Council appointed a sub-committee to examine the feasibility of such a project.

Six months later, the sub-committee submitted their report.[5] They recommended that the Council take a 40-year lease of 54 hectares (the approximate area of the present estate) from Michaelmas 1912. They calculated the expected income as follows:

200 playing members at 2gns	£420
100 lady members at lgn	£105
Visitors and reduced fees	£100
Total	£625

They allowed for the payment of interest on an initial capital outlay of £2,000. One of the 21 clauses was, 'No Sunday play to be allowed'. As a result of this report, the Council resolved to acquire land for a golf course on Bishopdown.[6] But they were advised that such a proposal was 'not within the powers of the Council'.[7] So the project was abandoned. Which is why golfers must now go to High Post or South Wilts to play.

The Council did acquire some of the Bishopdown land in 1927,[8] but no development took place then. In 1954 the Council purchased a further 24 hectares for £3,750;[9] the contract for the first council houses was awarded to J Prichard,[10] and building began in 1956. The south-western section, as far as Barrington Road, was completed in 1959; the north-eastern part in 1962.

Not all the estate was council housing: in 1956 the Council approved 17 houses for Salisbury (Self-Build) Housing Association Ltd.[11] And in 1973 Hardwill

Investments Ltd bought 1.5 hectares at the northern end of the estate for private development.[12] But the streets in that area (Hallum Close, Fison Walk and Woodvill Road) were not developed until 1979-80, by which time the Council had reclaimed responsibility for that part of the estate.

Before building had begun, Alderman Ernest Grant, a senior member of the Council and a former Mayor, wrote to the Housing Committee, 'suggesting that the streets on the Bishopdown Estate be named after well known Musical Composers.' But the Committee resolved to defer the matter until after development had started.[13] They later elected a street-naming sub-committee comprising Messrs Moore, Hoy, Annetts and Cane, Mrs Locock and Miss Bundy (now Lady Benson).[14] Their first suggestions were: Bishopdown Road, Link Way, Lime Kiln Road and Downland Road. In the event, the last two names were not used. The dropping of 'Lime Kiln Road' would have been regretted by the late Miss Evelyn Hart, who remembered:

> We children usually approached [Old Sarum] by the bridle road over the Lime Kilns - or Bishop's Down as these were sometimes called -which took us direct from Campbell Road to the old hill.[15]

At the next Housing Committee meeting, the sub-committee recommended that, 'in view of the association of the area with Bishops of Salisbury', the remaining 16 streets be named after bishops.[16] As we have noted, three more were added in about 1980.

These bishops' names were evidently pulled out of a hat without any consideration of their suitability. The sixteen bishops varied widely in their episcopates, from Burnet's 26 years to Fotherby's 11 months. Their characters varied from saintly to worldly: Jewel was definitely in the first category, whereas Hoadly was more polemical than episcopal. The first bishop of New Salisbury and founder of the new cathedral was not selected -but then, who would want to live in Poore Street'? On the other hand, the sub-committee selected William Anderson, who at the time was half-way through his 14-year episcopate.

It seems they simply selected some of the more euphonious names. Nobody bothered to check whether these bishops were worthy to be honoured. A slap-dash attitude seems to be evident also in the misspelling of the names of four bishops: Blythe, Hoadly, Jewel and Woodville. (But Woodvill Road was not named until about1980.)

After being so critical of the sub-committee, perhaps we can make amends by complimenting the member who suggested 'Lovett 'Green'. This is a play on lovat-green, a shade of tweed from Lovat near Inverness. Indeed the street sign at first spelt it 'Lovat Green', although 'Lovett Green' was the name in the minutes of the Housing Committee. At a meeting of that Committee in December 1960, the Town Clerk read a letter from a Mrs Barton, probably the widow of Canon

Walter Barton, who had been Bishop Lovett's examining chaplain, intimating that on her first visit to the Bishopdown Estate she was particularly pleased with the choice of names after Bishops of Salisbury, but was much puzzled by the spelling of the name 'Lovat' as she did not know of any bishop of that name, and wondered if the name should be 'Lovett'. So the Committee 'Resolved that the spelling...be amended to Lovett Green'.[17]

There are only two streets on Bishopdown which are not named after bishops: Bishopdown Road and Linkway (originally Link Way, as we have noted). The latter is a misnomer, for the road is a cul-de-sac. Possibly the original plans showed a' link to Bishopdown Road. The name could hardly be an allusion to the golf links which had been projected nearly half a century before.

Notes

[Salisbury City Records are in Wiltshire & Swindon Record Office (WSRO), class G23]

1   Benson R, and Hatcher H (1843) *Old and New Sarum, or Salisbury*, 1843, 816.
2   *Victoria history of Wiltshire* vol 6, 92.
3   Minutes of Salisbury Council, 6.7.1911.
4   Minutes of General Purposes Committee, 19.10.1911.

5   ibid 26.4.1912.
6   Salisbury Council, 2.5.1912.
7   ibid 6.6.1912.
8   Housing Committee, 14.6.1956.
9   ibid 8.7.1954.
10 ibid 8.12.1955.
11 General Purposes Committee, 22.3.1956.
12 Housing Committee, 15.3.1973.
13 ibid 19.1.1956.
14 ibid 12.7.1956.
15 Hart E (1984) *Before I Forget*, 60.
16 Housing Committee, 18.10.1956.
17 ibid 15.12.1960.

Notes on Contributors

Hugh Abel is the Chairman of Studio Theatre, and **Sue Johnson** is a local historian with a special interest in early Victorian Salisbury.

Peter Barrie graduated with a 1st class honours BA in Fine Arts Valuation Studies from Southampton Institute, and this paper is based on work undertaken for his dissertation. Besides 19th-century ceramics and an enthusiasm for the Gothic revival, he is a keen organist, and formerly played at St Mark's, where he discovered the parish records. He is deputy editor of *Carriage Driving Magazine* and lives in Salisbury.

Don Cross was born a Wiltshireman at Malmesbury and has lived for many years in both the north and south of the county. He saw war service and later, after University, became a teacher in London, Ringwood, Oxford and at Salisbury – the last as Senior Lecturer in Geography and Tourism at Salisbury College until retirement in 1989. A pioneer of industrial archaeology he founded the South Wiltshire society in 1965. A qualified Blue Badge Guide he is now Managing Director of his own Wessexplore Tourist and Training Services which he established in 1976.

John Elliott is an architectural historian who lives near Salisbury and teaches at the University of Reading. He specialises in the Victorian period.

Peter Fawcett is Henry Fawcett's great-great nephew. He is currently Managing Director and Company Chairman of The Tintometer Ltd, the world's market leader in colour and water testing equipment. The firm was founded by Joseph Lovibond, whose daughter Charlotte married Henry Fawcett's nephew. Peter regularly gives talks on the political ideas and achievements of Henry Fawcett, based upon a lifetime of research.

Peter Hart has strong links with Salisbury although he now lives in South Africa. He has completed an exhaustive study of Salisbury and Wilton street names, and has deposited copies of his research in Salisbury Local Studies Library and the Wiltshire & Swindon Record Office.

Steve Hobbs is an archivist at the Wiltshire & Swindon Record Office, whose edition of *Wiltshire Glebe Terriers* has just been published by the Wiltshire Record Society.

Carrie Smith is Assistant Editor of the *Victoria County History* in Wiltshire, and has recently been appointed County Editor in Gloucestershire. Her doctoral research focussed on crime and justice in medieval southern England.